Thirteen Pieces

of Unmatched Luggage . . .
and My Poodle!

Thirteen Pieces
of Unmatched Luggage…
and My Poodle!

Bernardo Puccio

William
Charles

10520 Wilshire Blvd.
#203
Los Angeles, CA 90024

Published 2019 by William Charles Press
Printed in the United States of America

21 20 19   1 2 3 4
ISBN 978-1-7337427-2-6
Library of Congress Control Number: 2019935206

This book is dedicated to the two people
who lovingly bookend my life.

To my guardian angel mother Maggie Puccio who gave
me the strength and imagination to be myself.

To my longtime partner and husband Orin Kennedy
who had the smarts to accept me as I am.

Thank you both for your wisdom, inspiration, and support.

⊰Table of Contents⊱

⫷ Introduction ⫸

Friday, May 23, 2014

I**T'S STRANGE HOW** one arrives at a defining moment in life. For some, it's through personal trauma, loss, or a near-death experience. For others, it is a place that is the trigger event to catharsis and change. I was at thirty-five thousand feet over the Atlantic on a flight to Paris when it hit me like a ton of bricks.

"Fuck it," I whispered to myself. "I'm going to write a book."

It would be a tell-all book that would hold nothing back. I'd spare no detail and there would be blood. I would take no prisoners; give no quarter; and feel no shame or incumbent remorse. Screw it! I would get Roman-evil in relating my adventures and would offer cautionary advice to readers who would dare share my experiences. That decision, while racing at over five hundred miles per hour in a virtual tin can, was made without regret or apology.

My journey was particularly amazing. I was a fragile boy from a small community called Ensley, located in Birmingham, Alabama. From that humble origin I became one of California's foremost interior designers. I walked with stars and luminaries who occupied the Golden Age of Hollywood. I tasted of every fruit and still craved more.

As the book began to take shape in my mind, images of my early existence began to form. My mother's face took on ethereal shape and substance. My beautiful mother, Maggie Puccio. That image evaporated suddenly, replaced by memories of my first lover—a cornerstone of erotic recollection that would, in large part, define my identity as a gay man without attendant fear and shame. In another microsecond of thought, the face of movie legend Lana Turner appeared...my one-time friend. In the span of a minute, like a dream that seems to last for hours, the transformative images of so many memories raced across my mind.

In retrospect, I remember being exhausted—but without the ability to find solace or peace in sleep. My mind began to wander. I knew I would not fail to recover the many details of my admittedly eventful existence. I guess that's what makes the reality of this book so marvelously damning. The insanity of my life to that point made the idea of a memoir stick. My God, it was like an immediate heroin high.

I grew up "gay" in the South and took a well-known married celebrity as my lover. Then after five years, I suddenly decided to leave everything behind and move across the country without a definitive plan. I managed to achieve an outstanding career, accompanied by a glamorous lifestyle, while living dangerously and surviving the AIDS epidemic and a life-threatening medical crisis. Finally, I was given the freedom to marry my partner of thirty-two years.

I was inspired. Mad, to be sure, but also rapturous in the pool of impending creativity and recall that I would commit to the written word. So there I was, in the cabin of a damned vehicle defying the laws of gravity and God (not necessarily in that order), excited to begin at, well, the beginning and persevere toward an end not yet clearly in sight.

Then it hit me—panic, nostalgia, and terror. Could I let myself go there, to glance back at it all, to relive both the good and the bad of my life? Really? Was I that brave? Nuts? Or both?

"How will this beautiful journey end?" I found myself asking aloud. A passing flight attendant stopped momentarily to look at me but then moved on as she realized I was in an incandescent state of self-reflection.

My life. My incredible, beautiful life that included celebrities, a thousand different loves, my life partner, Orin, and innumerable journeys across the globe. I had met the Beatles—me, a young fellow from the Deep South, wining and dining with the Fab Four. High above Earth as I reflected on my life, I could not help but wonder how it would all end. What man does not contemplate the where, how, and when of his death? The cliffhanger of oblivion or an unimaginable afterlife was, of course, the denouement of every existence. Having just turned seventy years old, I could not help but contemplate the inevitability of death and the ultimate finality to it all.

It was downright terrifying!

However, I had made the decision—and would keep it—to write this book. The confluence of emotions was wonderful and horrible, all at the same time. I know, that sounds ludicrous. How can such a situation bear the burden of both quiet ecstasy and impending terror? Answer, my friends: It is a delicious paradox. I would revel in it as I had reveled in life.

In that moment of mental exuberance, reality emerged. Who would read my book? I wondered. Who would care? Who would it entertain, sadden, amuse, or inspire? Would anyone really give a damn?

It was a daunting question at best. I decided I would not answer it at the moment.

Because, you see, the book was ultimately most important to me.

With that immediate sense of determination, I allowed my mind to wander to the great true love of my life: Orin Kennedy. Thinking of him immediately calmed me as it always did. He would turn seventy-five in one day. As he was five years older than me, thoughts of his mortality lingered in my mind as well. I glanced over at him, sitting quietly beside me, and wondered: Was he, too, afraid of death? Of course, Orin was scared.

Aren't you?

I chuckled suddenly. "Oh, shit, Orin's scared of everything!" He glanced at me and could sense with just his eyes that I was privately amused.

Orin.

We'd been through so much together. I try to remember only the good.

Thus, in part, the reason for our current European excursion. I'd been working too damned hard, having simultaneously finished several design projects. I had survived a very serious medical condition that necessitated an emergency operation, which miraculously saved my life. It was time for a vacation. My life had been blessed with love, passion, and professional success. Orin and I had been together for thirty-eight years. Why not celebrate it with a trip to the City of Lights? Another adventure!

I willed myself to cease the retrospection of seventy years and asked myself a more universal question. This book—this damned obsession at this point in my high-flying epiphany: What kind of legacy would it leave behind? My answer was unforgiving and emphatic: Simply tell the truth, Bernardo. No need to gild the lily.

The truth.

That is what my legacy would be. Unvarnished. Unsullied. Without makeup or mascara.

I would tell the story of a life well lived.

So, my dears, join me if you would. Come along for the ride. Let me regale you with glamour and magic, tragedy and fame. T.S. Eliot once said: "This is the way the world ends, not with a bang, but with a whimper."

Uh-uh. I'll take the bang every time!

⇥ 1 ⇤

The Light

February 2010

It's strange what one reflects upon when you think or suspect the end is near. I was suffering from end-stage liver disease and throwing up blood that would no longer clot. The stents I had received to help the passage of blood through my liver weren't working. My abdomen was filled with fluid that diuretics could no longer eliminate. However, I seemed to be in control of my thinking.

As I stared up into the blistering white light, it appeared that, for the first time in my life, events were unfolding far beyond my scope of control. Though in a state of almost unimaginable suffering, I was really pissed.

Then I heard the howl of the sirens like tortured electronic ghosts whining for release. They crept into the base of my spine, then shuddered through the rest of my body. Usually, you believe those horns of doom, rotating in a redolent hellish red, are for some other poor bastard, never you. While you may offer up a prayer for those unfortunate others presently suffering pain or near death, you nevertheless offer the age-old cry: "There but for the grace of God go I."

Until the sirens suddenly cease their infernal drone and you realize their song of Death is meant for you.

The light above me was blinding, otherworldly. Its brilliance momentarily frightened me. I had decided not to relinquish all control, not yet. On this night, I insisted on walking to our front door to get on the gurney. That would be all the activity I could muster this evening. After that, my fate was in the hands of others. I closed my eyes and prayed to my blessed mother and God to protect me.

I had been raised Catholic and had always held to the convictions of my religion. Though my private life had its share of self-indulgent pleasures, like sex and just plain having a good time, my faith had remained a bulwark of strength for my soul. I had turned to the Almighty many times before, but never more fiercely than in this moment of paralyzing fear in the face of the unknown.

Please, Jesus, not now. I need more time. I want more time.

By happenstance, I caught a glimpse of my own reflection against the stainless-steel medical case next to my stretcher. My skin was jaundiced, yellow as a malarial victim moments before expiration.

I felt overwhelming terror. Tears welled in my eyes. I could hear a moan escape my lips, brought forth from the deepest part of my sickened being—an unconscious primordial sound of unspeakable fear. I had never felt so hopeless, so consigned to an immutable sense of helplessness. I tried to fight back the tears I rarely showed, but in this, too, I had zero control. I'd become a whimpering infant.

God...oh, God...I was terrified.

I gripped my rosary, still draped around my palm, and wrenched my gaze away from my tortured reflection. I prayed.

Then, suddenly the paralytic fear began to dissipate. An almost preternatural peace enveloped me. I was impervious to the clatter of the opening and closing of the ambulance doors. I saw the white light again. I wasn't scared. I became aware that I was not alone. I felt the presence of God. I saw his face and he spoke to me. His voice was so kind. Softly, he said, "Don't be afraid, Bernard. This is not your time. I am not ready for you. Remember, you are loved." After that I heard the ambulance doors close.

The last words I heard were those of Orin. "I will meet you at the hospital." His eerie calm increased my sense of blissful peace.

The white light remained. I was in a near-euphoric state of solace and tranquility.

I allowed myself to descend into complete surrender; the light's dimming no longer so horrible a fear.

As the darkness enveloped me, I went back to a time of innocence and unquestioned love. As I lost consciousness, my last thought was that I knew I was with God and had his blessings and that he would see me through this life-or-death ordeal.

Time spiraled backward to a world composed of memories and ghosts of a past now existing only in dreams and history.

❧ 2 ❧
My Mother's Son

I WAS BORN BERNARD Puccio on February 24, 1944. No "O" at the end of Bernard. That little garnish would be added down the line, by movie star Lana Turner. My parents, Mike and Maggie Puccio, were first-generation Italians born in Birmingham, Alabama, to immigrant parents of Sicilian descent. I was the third child in what would eventually be a contingent of five: two brothers, two sisters, and myself. As the middle kid, I occupied the most difficult station. The two eldest, my sister Sarah and brother Joe, were respectively twelve and seven years older than me. Joe married young and thus became the first to leave the nest. Sarah and I would become very close.

Around the time of my entrance into this uncertain world, my father was called to register for the World War II draft. Because my mom was so close to giving birth to yours truly, my father was given a reprieve from battle to remain with his family. Shortly thereafter

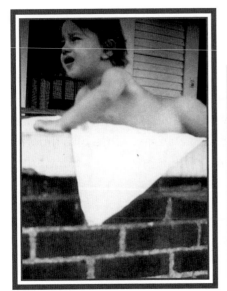

the age requirement for men to be drafted into the military was changed, much to the benefit of my father who was older than that new age limit.

My parents owned a grocery in Ensley, a large industrial neighborhood on the outskirts of Birmingham. They worked hard there to give their kids a good life. They did not fail. My dad, Mike Puccio, looked more like a Latin film star than a grocer. Most folks thought he resembled actor Cesar Romero, athletic, strong, and devilishly charming. He had a passion for sports that my brothers, but not I, shared with him. However, I took great pleasure realizing both my mom and dad depended on me when it came to running the store. In this, I excelled well beyond my siblings, who never worked in the family business. Ever.

Which brings me to my mother, Maggie Lorino Puccio. Suffice it to say that my mom was beautiful, inside and out. She was loving, warm, expressive, and empathetic. These virtues were not mine to appreciate alone—the townsfolk respected her unequivocally. Her customers fairly worshipped her and trusted her opinion on most matters.

The work ethic my parents instilled in me was a lifelong gift; working the business with them was never a chore, but rather a pleasure. I felt part of something important. The responsibility instilled in my favor filled me with pride and emboldened a spirit smoldering beneath the veneer of childhood innocence. At a very young age, I knew that the world beyond was filled with sadness and danger. Yet I had no fear of it. I welcomed it. I owe this sense of intrepidness to my parents, and I am forever grateful to them.

I loved my mom's company and adored her without reservation. She was my best friend. We all expect mothers to love their children, and my mother was no different with her kids. She loved us all equally. I also realized that, when it came to me, my mother actually *liked* me. She didn't show her love in the physical sense, but her trust and dependence on me to fulfill our family's needs, whether at home or at the store, showed me that she cared.

It's important to note that "liking" implied something fiercer than mere filial love. It denoted an innate understanding of character and self, which my mother clearly recognized in me. She saw in me something special from what this town could promise or offer. She saw in me what it has taken me seventy years to recognize at last: that I was destined to be different, and that I had an absolute right to be that individual. Being young, I did not know at the time the full ramifications of this birthright, but it was simmering like a slow boil even then.

Our grocery store was smack in the middle of the black community. No gentle way to put it—we were in the "hood," right and proper. We were white folk in what white folk considered the wrong part of town at a time in America's history when white and black communities were powerfully segregated. Yet we were accepted—no, we were a welcome element to the neighborhood. My nanny, Claudia Mae, who virtually raised me, was African American, and not once did I ever feel the spiritual or literal divide in our respective races. I felt only love— unselfish, unbridled, motherly love.

I had issues, of course. Older family members referred to my physical appearance as *faccia bella*—beautiful face. I look back now with humility and eschew that Italian expression.

But beyond my gentle exterior there lay a fragility few knew about at the time. I was wracked by asthma and allergies. I was a weak kid, though I had a boy's natural resilience to the rough and ready. Even still, my mother was always there to offer protection—hell, it was more like she was enforcing militaristic Secret Service–like security for my well-being. She recognized my "difference" and decided early on to guard it with the formidable will of a grizzly bear protecting her cubs.

Another overriding reason for my mother's devotion to me, perhaps above that of my siblings, was due to my many maladies and a delicate disposition physically and emotionally. I needed Mom around a lot. She needed me around a lot as well.

Papa Ben and me

I was named Bernard, after my maternal grandfather, who I shall refer to hereafter affectionately as Papa Ben. Ben Lorino was a strong character. He was an adept and clever businessman. Most importantly, he was a truly good man. He owned the original Tuxedo Junction in Ensley, which at the time was significant as it represented a dance hall, a bar, and a popular hit song of 1940. I enjoyed Papa Ben's company immensely and the feeling was mutual. I was the favorite of all the kids in the old man's eyes. Don't ask me why. Maybe it was that "different" gene that made it so. I ate up the attention he showered upon me.

Interesting side note to Papa Ben's past: All was not perfect in Oz—and the Wizard had a few skeletons behind the curtain. In the late 1930s, my grandfather and family were returning from a church event in a two-door car. During those years, Papa Ben always carried a revolver on his person, loosely held in his pant belt. As he exited the vehicle that fateful day, the heavy door swung back toward him and knocked the gun free from his belt holster. The gun discharged and the bullet slammed into the skull of Papa Ben's young nephew, a boy of around ten. The bullet achieved its devilish task. The boy was dead before he hit the ground.

It was a freak accident, the magnitude of which held the small town's headlines for a week. Papa Ben never fully recovered from the incident, as my mother related many times. The incidentals of each family tale were riveting for me. We all carry the history of our fathers and fathers' fathers deep in our genes and consciousness. We are haunted by such history and fascinated as well. I was more enthralled than most by my family's history.

I was perhaps more advanced in my thinking than other children of my age, with whom I had nothing in common. I state this with all modesty inasmuch as I don't pretend to be some Olympian thinker. It's just that I perceived circumstances around me, and people, in a way that normal kids simply did not. I got it. I simply accepted this as being "just the way it was." Plus I was smart! After I was promoted twice in grammar school, Mother went to my teacher and said, "No more! I want my son to graduate with children his own age."

With this relatively peaceful acceptance of self, I continued to enjoy Papa Ben's stories as well as those of my mother. As I matured, I grew to exceedingly depend upon my mother's company and support, especially on those nights when Dad would head out to play cards with the guys and drink. I had few friends besides Mom. Sensing my difference, she never tried to mitigate it with attempts at turning me into a more normal standard of a child society might more readily accept. She was wiser than this by far. She realized that my off-the-beaten-path disposition might not be as easy to assimilate for our small-town world. Yeah, I was a challenge for Mom, but she never made me feel that burden, not for a moment.

Let me give you an example. My favorite toy was not a truck or a soldier or a baseball. No, my favorite plaything was my mother's wedding dress adorned with beads. I had found it one day in her cedar chest. In the Italian tradition, keepsakes of great importance to a young bride were consigned to a hope chest, to be passed on to a daughter, God willing, or, at the very least, the next generation. Mom never liked her all-lace wedding dress, which in those days the groom's parents bought. She wanted satin. Also Mom didn't care for her tough Italian mother-in-law. Neither did I. The woman had a tendency to squeeze my face each time we met.

Parent's Wedding

So, there I was, almost daily, playing with Mom's wedding dress. Well, not just playing, but also deciding to wear the damn thing. It was all lace and fit relatively well on my lank physique. As fate would have it, my mother finally caught me prancing around in her wedding gown, in front of a mirror, pretending to be a bride. Instead of berating me for such outlandish behavior, she allowed me to continue to play. I think she became tired of telling me not to wear the dress. However, she did say, "Only play with the dress when I'm there!"

My mother was a clever woman. She set down ground rules for our little excursions into fantasy land—a land where her young son could perform variations of *Swan Lake* in her wedding gown—and she was emphatic about how I was to conduct myself in public (and in private) to secure the sanctity of our little secret.

I respected her guidance as sacrosanct. We would play house on many a day and enjoyed this alternative reality we had created for each other, but we were also vigilant in our presentation. For example, when we heard Dad or someone coming home, we hurriedly broke down our world. In my case, I disrobed accordingly from the trappings of matrimony and assumed my human self again for the general public. It became a game for us—one that was ours and ours alone to enjoy.

Years later, my mother and I found ourselves in the kitchen one night as usual. She said to me in a gentle voice: "Bernard, I want to teach you how to walk like John Wayne—not Lana Turner." This was years before *La Cage aux Folles* was conceived. Receptive to virtually anything new in life, especially from my mother, I opened myself up to the experiment. Thus, I began my training in "Duke-a-fying" my walk, to the point of some distraction for my mother, as I believe at last I got it down pretty good. I look back now in wry amusement as several years later I would be with my then good friend Lana Turner, chatting and drinking with her—and watching her walk as I had walked like her so many years earlier!

As for John Wayne's strut, I did the best I could. I was a tough bastard and could play the part.

While my mother was loving and doting, she could also be critical. I accepted this as a matter of course and did my best to always do better in her eyes. I wanted to exceed her expectations of me at all times. This was the measure of our mutual resolve. As time passed, anything that she asked me to do, I endeavored to do my best. This included the daily chores and errands.

Take shopping, for instance. Working in the grocery all day, Mother did not have the time to go shopping. She sent me downtown with a precise list of household items and clothing to buy for the family. She trusted my taste. Besides I enjoyed the experience. It gave me pleasure and some extra bucks in my pocket. As a result, I became her go-to person in the family—the guy to depend upon in most matters.

I was ten when my sister Sarah got married. Robert Vetrano was an intelligent, good-looking man, who worked as a salesman for Jergens skin care products. I admired him so. I even took his name when I was confirmed: Bernard Robert Puccio. They were young and very much in love. No expense was spared on their big Italian wedding. My parents were very happy.

Sarah was such an important part of my life. Her gentle and understanding nature made me feel secure and special. She was very sensitive and so different from my other siblings—extremely shy and not at all outgoing like the rest of us. Sarah was smart and I appreciated her company. We enjoyed shopping and having lunch together. Aside from my mom, she was my best friend. I missed her when she married and left home, but I was thrilled to receive her bedroom.

Before that I shared a room with my younger brother, Phillip. We didn't get along. He was my opposite in most ways, tough and always in trouble. My baby sister, Marietta, nine years younger than myself, rounded out the family. Marietta was the most beautiful baby imaginable, with curly brown hair and pretty blue eyes like my mother. I recall how happy my folks were that another girl was in the family. She was a surprise, to be sure, but a welcome one. I was particularly thrilled with the new addition. Marietta became my living doll. I adored her. I was very close to both my sisters.

As my mother worked incessantly at the store, I became, happily, Marietta's primary caretaker. Perhaps it was my maternal instinct. Even though we had a maid, I was Marietta's private watchdog and insured she was cared for in every way. When I was a teenager, Marietta would have her girlfriends come over and I'd fix all of them lunch and we'd enjoy many good times together.

The store was open six days a week until 7:00 p.m. At 6:00 p.m. every day, my mom would phone home and tell me to head to the store. I'd walk the two blocks and secure the cash from the register, put it into a paper bag, which I tied around my leg, and then run home with the money. We did this to ensure that no robbery would take place against my parents as they closed shop. It was a smart tactical decision and a routine that remained unbroken. I look back now at that seemingly simple task and take pride in it. I was the family treasurer—at least in my perception of things. My dad would point out with pride that in all those years of running his store he was never robbed. This went on until I turned sixteen years old and got my driver's license. Then, I began doing all the banking for the store by driving to the bank, which I loved doing.

Spending time in the family store was fun and not just my duty. See, everyone in town comes to know you and you come to know them as well. The store itself became a kind of town meeting hall. Working there gave me invaluable experience and a strong work ethic. I learned how to run a business, oversee inventory, and understand the positive aspects of money. Working in the store never interfered with my private life. I made friends in high school, the closest being my cousin Joe Anthony, and had the freedom to do what I wished. My mother never denied me these privileges. Life was good.

Early in my teens, I wasn't dating. I didn't know that I was gay. I didn't even know what the word "gay" meant. Attempting to fit in, I started dating a lovely Italian girl named Rita. We remained friends for many years thereafter without any romantic notions ever attached.

Just good old-fashioned high school boyfriend and girlfriend.

Which suited me just fine.

❧ 3 ❧

A Life Well Lived

February 2010

AS I LAY in my bed at Los Angeles' Cedars-Sinai facility—feeling cold and scared—I reflected back on those carefree times in Ensley. How long ago that seemed and it was. Now, exhausted from my illness and after several hospital emergency trips, I had become gravely ill. Even so, as I awaited death or some alternative (no doubt radical), I knew I had to make some critical decisions. It was February 10, 2010. I'll never forget that date. Never. After countless consultations with so many specialists, the consensus was unanimous: I only had a short time to live.

Unless I agreed to a liver transplant.

After being rushed to the hospital by ambulance one night a few weeks earlier, bleeding internally, I became scared beyond all reason. The Grim Reaper was near and I could feel his cold hand upon me. Orin shared my terror.

Dr. Graham Woolf, my gastroenterologist, had been treating me for years. The mention of a liver transplant was not a news flash. My proverbial nine lives were shrinking. I had always remained vehemently against a transplant, but being obstinate in this matter did not alter my reality. Without the transplant, I'd soon be dead. Period. End of story. In a way, I had lived well and maybe, in the big scheme of life, it was simply time to go. I had stopped drinking seven months earlier in hopes of bringing an end to this physical horror. It had not. My liver was irreparably damaged by cirrhosis.

From a physiological perspective, my body had swollen terribly and could no longer expel fluids. I was filled with toxins. Blood failed to flow through my liver properly, and I was given to regularly throwing up blood.

Though terrified, I was determined to attend to necessary personal business should the worst finally happen. With Orin constantly by my side, I made out a new will, even while enduring continual blood tests and checkups. Orin, this articulate, kind gentleman I had met so many years earlier, was terrified. He tried to remain calm for me and generally succeeded. Inside, I knew, he was dying with me.

My sister Marietta was worried sick. She lived three thousand miles away in Birmingham and felt helpless.

I realized I was putting these people through a living hell. There was nothing they could do. Orin was suffering a slow torture watching me die. I felt that I could do something to possibly prevent what was about to happen should I choose to not be so selfish in my obstinacy and refusal to get the transplant! Or was it really the fear of dying that was prompting me to reconsider my decision?

With this in mind, one morning I awoke and looked to Orin.

"I want to go to Dr. Woolf's office," I said.

Walking was now very difficult. A kind nurse, whom I had come to like immensely, came by to assist us. She wheeled me in to speak to Dr. Woolf.

"What are you in for today, Bernardo?" the doctor asked.

I raised my head weakly and replied, "You know the transplant you've been talking about for years? Well, I think it's time."

Both Orin and Dr. Woolf regarded me in clear shock. Orin, I could tell, was immensely relieved.

"What changed your mind, Bernardo?" Dr. Woolf asked.

I took a deep breath. "I can't put Orin through this anymore."

Dr. Woolf, to his immense credit, wasted no time. He made critical calls and immediate arrangements to accommodate my request. I did not look back. I had made the decision to give life another chance and, whatever the outcome of the transplant, I would be in God's hands.

I felt I made the right decision.

This was a turning point—one of those moments in your life that stays etched and indelible in your mind and soul. This was a biggie, no doubt about it. You remember every pivotal moment leading up to such a decision and you relive it repeatedly. Details remain magnified; for instance, I still remember the smell of leather from Dr. Woolf's office chair. I still remember Orin's tears.

Dr. Woolf explained to Orin and me that an initial evaluation would have to be performed here in the hospital. It was scheduled for February 24—ironically, my birthday. The examination consisted of being poked, prodded, and tested from head to toe to determine if my body would survive such an invasive procedure as a liver transplant and was otherwise in good health.

Orin and the hospital team helped me with support and love, as best they could. In my rare moments of lucidity during this period, my thoughts floated back to those early days in Alabama with my mother in the kitchen, safe in our private sanctuary. From that point, I would then commute my psyche to my early manhood, my "coming of age" as it were.

Suddenly, at those times, the hospital became a temporary nightmare.

Back I would go and remember better and transformative times.

⤜4⤛

Retrospective

BY THE TIME I entered high school, I was fully aware of my innate love for music, art, and the movies. I was attracted to everything beautiful, obsessed really, especially regarding clothes, jewelry, and home furnishings. Eventually, this led to my giving our family home a makeover. I repainted it, changed fabrics, and did anything else I could to beautify our house. No one seemed to object.

I didn't necessarily understand how this activity would translate into a viable professional future, but I didn't care. I was having fun. Moreover, how could I begin to fathom what an interior designer was or did? Up to my high school days, I knew only the life of a merchant in a family store. I was skilled in business, but had no clue what I was truly destined to do. It was kind of like my personal life—I had friends but never any love affairs as yet.

I didn't know anything about gay life. However, I knew it was both strange and exciting that I found certain men sexually attractive—but never a woman. During these formative years, I simply went along with my group of friends, and generally had a great time while continuing to work in the family store. My mother, as always, asked me to do special errands for her—particularly, shopping for the family and paying bills. To me, it was simply an enjoyable set of diversions.

As a senior in high school, I signed up for a challenging regimen of piano, voice, and music appreciation classes at the Birmingham Conservatory of Music. During my eight months of studies at the C of M, I had the pleasure of studying voice with Andrew Gainey, renowned baritone with the New York City Opera, and met Teresa Rinaldi, Miss Alabama 1961, who was studying piano. I wanted to try everything. I knew my life would be involved in some way with entertaining or working with the public. Eventually, I realized that none of the conservatory's offerings were for me. I simply wasn't good at any of them. While I enjoyed learning, it wasn't going to lead to a career.

Upon graduation from high school, I decided to enroll in Alverson Draughon Business College, taking classes in bookkeeping, typing, and psychology. I already had practical experience in running the family business, and believed that experience, coupled with more knowledge, was enough to guarantee success. The compass I had created for myself to True North seemed firmly entrenched in my life's journey.

This experience suited me well for the future, but I had no passion for commerce, either. Decorating, however, came so easily to me. I decided in short order that being a decorator, as it was called back in the day, was what I wanted. I did not consider design and a sound understanding of economics to be mutually exclusive. In my mind, they were critically interconnected if I wished to succeed on a financial level with my dream career.

With this issue firmly understood, I was determined to make my dream a reality. My life seemed on the right path. I didn't understand where this decisiveness would lead, but I loved pondering the great possibilities ahead of me. After all, isn't that the joy of being young— to love the newness of endless opportunities and challenges?

Then suddenly my world shattered into a million pieces.

Early one morning, I heard a resounding and devastating crash. Somehow, I realized immediately that my mother had fallen. When I found her lying on the floor, seconds seemed like hours. She was unresponsive. I knew something was terribly wrong. I called 911 and then my father at the store, telling him to come home fast. From that moment on, everything became a horrible blur of unreality.

In less than fifteen minutes the ambulance and paramedics arrived, and the family gathered to head for the hospital. Part of me simply couldn't wrap my head around what was happening. My mother, so beautiful and seemingly impervious to health issues, had suffered a massive stroke that paralyzed her completely. I was stunned, as was the rest of the family.

I took charge from that point on, becoming the liaison between the doctors and the family concerning my mother's future care. In all humility, I never cracked or folded under the pressure. My father had the store to run—I ran the house and family. I was flattered that the doctors told my dad and grandparents how amazing it was that I could run the ship so effectively. I believed I was doing no more than what was expected and required of me in this time of crisis. On the rare occasions when someone asked me how I was holding up, I would invariably reply, "Don't worry about me." So, they didn't. I was an oak in their eyes, and those who radiate strength incur little concern as to their well-being. My grandparents and friends considered it natural for those possessed of such courage. I adored my mother and did not want to leave her. I spent hours sitting at the hospital.

In my mind, I just had to see that my mother was cared for in the best possible way. If I was to honor this incredible woman who had allowed me to be myself, then it was incumbent upon me to see her get well, no matter what.

At the time, I was seventeen years old; my baby sister, Marietta, was eight, my younger brother, Phillip, thirteen. My older brother and sister had already married and moved away, so it was up to me to guide my siblings and support my father. My mother, it was determined, would need twenty-four-hour care. Tragically, my father never really accepted that his wife had fallen so ill. He resumed his work and routine as if nothing out of the ordinary had occurred. He simply couldn't deal with it. I'm sure he was devastated, but he just couldn't show emotion.

My mother was hospitalized for a long time. She was unable to walk and would never speak again. It was devastating for the entire family. We had been so totally dependent on Mother who had complete control of the family. I had little time to grieve for the loss of my mother's voice in my life. That very first person I called when needing advice, the person whom I might have shared my achievements with in the future, that loving individual was no longer in existence. It was a hard reality, but one I accepted with customary resolve. I didn't feel sorry for myself—I just wanted Mother to be okay.

Fortunately, I had help in this area. We had maids who came in to assist with the housekeeping, and Mother had Ethel, a wonderful caregiver who assisted her in learning how to walk and assume some semblance of outward normality. Also, we had various nurses come in for physical therapy. I would take my mother to the store and the beauty salon. It fell to me to mind her medications. Our roles as parent and child had changed. Those days of her holding my hand in times of trouble had been turned upside down. It broke my heart to see her so helpless—and now, dependent on me for so much. It was equally gut-wrenching to witness her slow decline. She was at the hospital constantly.

After one year my mother improved with physical therapy and was able to walk again, but she never regained her speech. The stroke had destroyed her vocal cords. I tried helping her to talk, but she never spoke again. I was the only one who could understand what she wanted to say—we were that close. Even after so many years, I still would love to hear her voice—I can't even remember what she sounded like. It is a total blank.

These two years were hellish. It took a visual as well as emotional toll on me that I didn't really understand at the time. I withered down to a ninety-eight-pound kid who never stopped moving for the sake of the family, mostly tending to Mother.

Concurrent to this real-time horror in life, I was beginning to explore my sexuality as a gay man. This journey brought with it a great sense of vulnerability that could have led me to bad decisions and situations. It was the early '60s. I was careful and discreet about being gay. The subject was not openly discussed. Many of my gay friends married and lived unhappy lives. I was lucky! I followed my intuition and lived my life exactly the way I wanted. No one would tell me what to do! Nothing bad ever happened to me.

My first "gay" experience was with a man who lived in our neighborhood. He approached me and I accepted his proposal to have sex with him. I liked it. Immensely. I began to enjoy numerous sexual encounters that somewhat took the edge off the chaos of my irreconcilable family reality.

One night while frequenting a local bar with some friends, a buddy of mine named Bobby leaned over to me.

"Hey, there's a guy at the bar who would like to meet you," he said.

"Yeah, really? Who is he?" I asked.

Bobby pointed at a fair-haired fellow across the way. "Him. He's a DJ. Jim Taber, a real celebrity in the rock circuit."

I shrugged indifferently. "Not interested. No thank you."

Bobby shrugged as well at my easy dismissal of this local "star." I don't know why but I've never been easily impressed by anyone or anything. Something about the way Bobby described this guy gave me a gut feeling it was "all wrong."

Again, the DJ dude offered me a drink. I again resisted his preamble invite.

Finally, the DJ came over to my table.

"Why didn't you want to meet me?" he asked.

I sensed most people didn't say no to him often.

"I'm not interested," I replied dryly. It did not occur to me that my very clear no to his advances might make me even more appealing to a guy who probably was used to always getting his way. We began talking, though I don't know why. As I look back, I think, in an odd way, I welcomed the conversation. I was distraught at my mother's condition, not knowing how much longer she would live. I was feeling broke in so many ways. I felt I had lost everything, my mother, my best friend.

This Jim fellow presented an enticing distraction and he began to intrigue me. He was good-looking and obviously well known. The thought of maybe being with someone who genuinely cared for me provided a sense of comfort and solace. I didn't wish to be lonely anymore as I was now alone on so many levels. He was interested in me. He knew what he wanted and he wanted me and it felt good.

I was to learn that Jim was program director at WSGN-Birmingham. He had an outgoing personality with an incredibly strong voice, and was responsible for bringing a new sound and look to Birmingham radio. Jim had a line-up of DJs he named The Good Guys, and had lots of innovative ideas and promotions, including the Pick Hit of the Week. He adored what he did. He was also well educated, having graduated college in Denver, Colorado.

After several dates I began to fall in love with Jim. I was so alone. I really needed him and he adored me. Soon after he declared pointedly: "I'm going to marry you. You're the most beautiful man I've ever seen. I'm going to divorce my wife and marry you someday."

I half smiled at this bold disclosure, not really taking him too seriously—though something told me he truly meant what he said, or at least thought he did.

Jim Taber was a married man when we met. Being married and having male lovers on the side was a definite social no-no. Homosexuality wasn't discussed in those days, at least not in polite company. Sometimes this meant hiding behind a wife—one was

forced into such a situation to keep up appearances of "straightness."
It was grossly unfair, but that was life at the time. Coming out as
gay was so very difficult during the '60s, especially being a radio
and TV personality. No one wanted to be openly gay. Although Jim
and I attended every event together—and eventually lived together,
which everyone knew—it was just one of those things that was not
discussed in public. After Jim met me, he filed for divorce, and I
never met his wife and she never met me. She accused him of having another woman. She also was very stupid, and when she left their
home together, she didn't take any of the silver items in the cabinet.
These were their wedding gifts and were worth thousands. When Jim
saw this, he looked at me and said, "It's all yours." I still have all of it.
I don't know how anyone could be that stupid.

⇥5⇤

No Room for Me
and Your Mother

JIM TABER HAILED from Dallas, Texas. If I were to be with him, this enticing package came with his overbearing, redheaded Auntie Mame of a mother. She was a very interesting lady, to put it kindly. It's the only benign euphemism I can find for her, even now, without sounding resentful and bitchy.

Mable Taber adored her only son and spoiled him to death. I believed it was normal for a mother to do so, especially to an only child. However, I was the one living with Jim, not her. Mable was controlling, with a jealous and disturbing disposition. In her eyes Jim was perfect.

Mable was a collector of exotic pets and had killed the animals herself. Leopards, minks, a zebra—you name it, she had it. The family, you see, was in the safari business and this entailed, of course, wholesale murder of almost every animal that ever existed on the Serengeti. Jim's mom and her second husband gave lectures and wrote articles and books on hunting and safaris. They did not want to accept the fact that Jim and I were anything more than friends—even though we would go to their house together for Christmas and they had full knowledge that we lived together. It was weird. Of course, they knew—Jim loved me so much there was no way he could hide it. He really didn't care what they thought. I was his life.

So, as you've already probably guessed, these were eccentric and wealthy Texans of the old-school era. I liked them well enough, except for their predilection for big-game hunting, but not enough to motivate me to exist in a world too close in proximity to them. There's my Southern charm for you.

It came to my attention at length that Jim was heir to a fortune. What I didn't know was that he had already received a considerable portion of said inheritance from his father, who was killed in a plane crash. Because of this inheritance, Jim owned his own plane, a Cessna 183, and he loved to fly it. I wondered at the time if this was some sort of defiant hubris to the universe—a kind of thumbing his nose at whatever gods may be that practically cried, "I'm going to fly even if you killed my father!"

I never asked him point-blank on this matter. Honestly, as far as his lifestyle went, I loved it. We were jetsetters in every sense of the word—on the "scene" with anyone who was anyone. At a time when rock music was introducing some of the most iconic bands of the century, we were at the epicenter of history. I dug it completely.

I loved it for other reasons as well. I had been so accustomed to taking care of other people for so long, it was good to be taken care of for once. Not only taken care of—spoiled rotten. Jim and I would fly guests to dinner in other states. It was truly that extravagant. I even learned to be a co-pilot, and although I never became good at it, it was still quite cool. It was never lost on me that I was living life much larger than most people could ever dream. In retrospect, because I was so young, I thought it was natural. I dove into this lifestyle as if

I'd been accustomed to it from birth. Over the course of our romance, Jim and I flew coast-to-coast many times as well as to other parts of the country. Jim showed me a fairy-tale world.

Then, of course, there were all the rock stars!

As a DJ for a radio station in Birmingham, Jim allowed me to meet all the relevant rock stars of the 1960s—the Rolling Stones, Chubby Checker, the Bee Gees, Everly Brothers, and others. None of these celebrities impressed me. Jim felt differently, but he was a rock music disc jockey, so that was his business. We had some wonderful times with these entertainers. (Interesting to note, there were no female recording artists.) Jim hosted many "sock hops"—that's what they called informal sponsored dance events featuring popular music of the time. I always went along for the ride. I understood my role. I was the trophy boy—Jim loved showing me off.

There would come a day when I would not be so receptive to not taking center stage, but those days were not upon me yet. For the time being, I enjoyed being showered with gifts and treated like a prince. I knew Jim really loved me—and I liked that, as well. I was also terribly inexperienced as a gay man. Up to this point, it had been all about exploration. I had no gay role models or other points of reference.

I assumed what I had with Jim was the way of all gay couples. I had become dependent on Jim, and while I loved him, this aspect made me uncomfortable. Being the "kept" boyfriend was a component I never dreamed of—nor was it inherent with my personal nature of resisting any kind of suppression. I had no idea how to truly behave as a trophy boyfriend.

For now, I was just playing it by ear.

I would do so for a while longer because, in truth, Jim was every-thing to me. I was enormously grateful to him for all the blessings he bestowed upon me.

However, I was beginning to feel confined and I wanted to grow.

⚒6⚒

After the Pain

FOR A MICROSECOND, my eyes opened, or so I believed. As I was wheeled into some nebulous room in the ICU, the world went terribly dark again. I saw no bright lights guiding me nor did I hear prayers to the Virgin Mother. I do believe I occupied some alien space between life and death—an anteroom to existence and oblivion. I felt no immediate fear—that had diminished, at least for the time being. I was simply exhausted. I'd worked so hard all my life, devoting myself to beauty and excellence. If God now wanted me to rest, I would not fight the Almighty on this; my faith in Him was great—I was completely in his hands.

He had given me so much. I had danced around the world and dined with celebrities. I was a well-known interior designer. I had known success. I had known great love—more than once. I had wanted to be the best at what I did and I believe I succeeded in this endeavor. Even as my skin went horribly yellow, I remained alert, a fighter. I had not embraced the idea of death or surrendered to it. I was going to stay for the duration and God help anyone who stood in my way.

These thoughts coalesced in my mind as I was wheeled about, and my thoughts again went down that Yellow Brick Road of memory to a time when I had to deal with the very real issue of the world's perception of me as a gay man.

It was fall 1964. My association with Jim up to this point had been wisely discreet, for both Jim's protection and mine. In those days, should word get out that we were a "couple," only trouble could follow. In my young and relatively innocent experience of such matters, I had no clue what would happen if everyone knew I was gay. Certainly my sister Sarah knew and always had. My mother, without doubt, was only too aware of my sexual orientation. Most of my family tacitly accepted my lifestyle. I was safe. I felt no threat of some terrible exposure.

In time, of course, rumors flew about that I was gay, and it became common knowledge. Yet I never faced hostility from anyone in town, nor from my peers and retinue of close friends. I got my first ugly dose of homosexual bigotry *not* from a stranger, but from my own brother, Joe.

It had been a rough time for me with my mother being so ill. I ran the house, oversaw her post-stroke care, and monitored her recovery from hip surgery after a fall. The stress was unimaginable.

One evening, Jim and I decided to go to a movie, as we had done so many times before. I took great joy in analyzing the sets and studying the jewelry the actresses wore. I imagined myself at lunch with such movie stars as Elizabeth Taylor and Lana Turner, wondering what we would talk about. Little could I imagine then that one day I would indeed be sharing meals with these two giants of film history.

I forget exactly what the picture was that we saw this night, but we had a wonderful evening. As we left the theater, I suddenly felt someone grab my elbow; I let out a scream and turned to see my brother Joe, eyes blazing and a snarl on his lips. How did he track me down? Joe was married and living on his own at the time.

"Come with me!" he growled.

To avoid complete public humiliation, I decided to go with Joe and said goodnight to Jim, who appeared shocked. Joe pulled me toward him. I realized this was my brother—generally irrational with an anger that was unpredictable. He was simply too violent for me to lash out; I didn't dare.

"You better not see that guy again!" he yelled, still pulling me. I attempted to resist, but rather feebly against his force.

This was a truly frightening moment for me and represented a turning point in my life.

Joe dragged me for what seemed like a mile. I was furious—I wanted to kick his mean-spirited ass. How dare he interfere in my life! Patrons from the theater, entering or exiting, stared at us. It was beyond embarrassing; it was humiliating. My brother then threw me into the passenger seat of his car, raced around to the driver's side, got in, and tore into me.

"You can't keep seeing this guy. This is wrong, Bernard!"

I turned to my brother with a ferocity that I could see momentarily startled him.

"Joe, you can't tell me what to do! Who the hell do you think you are? Let me out of this damn car!"

"Faggot!" he shouted.

"Asshole!" I retorted. "Who gave you the fucking right to tell me what to do?"

Joe turned the car's ignition on and sped down the street, like a demon, too fast for me to open the door and jump out lest I kill myself in the attempt. We hit some road bumps and this jostled my seat, only increasing my anger. At the same time, I was afraid because of his angry and erratic behavior.

At length, though, I had enough. I screamed at him, "Joe, let me out of this car. Right now! I'm jumping out!"

"You're not jumping out anywhere!" he yelled back. "I did you a favor. You can't be hanging around that guy. People will think things. Besides, he's married!"

I thought of the absurdity of the statement. I think I might have let out an unconscious chuckle at how inane my brother sounded. He continued to vent.

"You are never to see him again. You hear me, Bernard?"

I stared at him with an icy malevolence that surprised even myself. In that moment, I could have killed him. I was a tough son of a bitch, to be sure, and I realized right there and then that I would never let anyone tell me what to do. Ever.

"Take me home now," I said quietly.

These would be the last words I would speak to my brother for many years. We were from different worlds. Reality was—we were never close. As time passed, I felt bad, not only for myself, but also for my jerk of a brother. It was difficult for me to sustain my resentment and anger toward him.

I remembered another reason I had resented Joe. He had always upset my mother, and she constantly covered for him to protect his wild behavior. I also remember doing my homework at the kitchen table while he constantly went out of his way to annoy me. I would write with an ink pen and he would push my hand incessantly; at one point, I got so mad that, after the third push, I stabbed him in the hand. Boy, did he ever scream. I'm sorry to confess that both my brothers bullied me. I think they were jealous of my relationship with my mother.

Joe's car pulled up in front of the house and I got out, not looking back. He hollered some nasty words at me, but I did not acknowledge him. I entered the house, still livid, and let the door slam shut behind me. Who was he to tell me what to do?

Once in my own room, I took private counsel with myself. That was the last straw!

I could no longer remain in this environment. I had to escape. I called Jim and told him I was leaving home and I was moving in with him that night. Joe had done such irreparable harm that I knew I could not stay. Not even for my mother. I packed a bag and left that very night. Jim took me in and I now felt safe. The change, I realized, was a long time coming and inevitable. That frightful night represented the final blow.

Tragically, that same September, shortly after my enraged departure, my precious mother passed away in the hospital. The year was 1964 and I was twenty years of age.

The death of Maggie Puccio devastated not just me, but my entire family. It also had an impact on our community in ways I could not expect. Though the inner family suffered in indescribable ways—the matriarch of our collective being torn from our midst—the town as a whole felt her departure. At her funeral, there were folks from every background whose lives had been touched by my mother. An entire city, black and white, showing up to pay respects to my mother was a beautiful testament to a great lady. I was (and am) so proud to be her son.

Though my immediate family was near, I was truly alone, except for Jim. He made my life a little easier. He continued to care for me, love me, worship me, and spoil me. He was my protector and lover—my everything.

Change was in the air.

Not that day of the funeral. Rather, it was like a gathering storm— one that would hit me and those around me like a nuclear blast.

⇥ 7 ⇤

Carving Out a New Life

HAVING MOVED INTO Jim's apartment, I began my life with Jim as a couple. I was twenty years old and Jim was twenty-four.

I decorated it with verve and style, adding a new beauty to the place that amazed even me. No expense was spared. Jim just told me to have a good time and do what I wanted. I delivered, as requested.

Prior to meeting Jim, I worked at Birmingham's premier department store, Loveman's, in window display, organizing furniture and accessories. This position gave me a good learning experience of colors, fabrics, and period furnishings and recognition. I loved this job. A few months later the store manager offered me a much better position as a salesman in the furniture department.

After two years I joined the staff of Birmingham Wholesale, the finest furniture store in Birmingham, where my career took off. The best designer in the South trained me. She took me under her wings and taught me everything for almost four years. What a great learning experience I received from Gertrude Adams, a real tough lady who just loved me. She always said I had better taste than she did.

I could now create and design like no one they had seen before. I worked there until I left Birmingham.

Jim's career achieved a new high—he was bigger than ever as a celebrity DJ. He was the best at what he did. When he was on the air as a broadcaster, he was in heaven. He loved his job and did it so comfortably. Being from Dallas, he had an incredible deep voice and a slight Texas accent. A true Texan in every way, Jim always said everything is big in Texas, and believe me, when he did anything, he did it in a big way—especially when it came to me. Money was no object, and we lived life on a grand scale. Jim had his own plane, the finest car, and yes, his prize possession—me. He showered me with gifts and his love until I felt smothered and wanted to fly on my own.

We both had successful careers. I was in decorating and he was in broadcasting. Our success was a rhapsody of pure joy and adventure. We went everywhere together.

In September 1964 we flew to Dallas to attend a rock concert. As Jim worked at one of the most prestigious radio stations of the time, WSGN-AM Birmingham, he had access to the best venues and singing groups. This particular night we went to Memorial Stadium to see the newest sensation, an English group called The Beatles. Yes. Them! They autographed a poster of themselves for me but, to be frank, back then, I didn't really understand their appeal. They were gaining national, if not global, recognition at the time, but being a small-town boy, I didn't understand their popularity at all.

When Chubby Checker arrived on the scene, it was a whole different story. Chubby represented great dance music and I was a dancing queen! I love to dance to this very day. At Italian weddings, I was always the one whom the older ladies loved to partner with. "Come dance, Bernard," was my Italian wedding love call from the women! I would always oblige them—I'd show them the Twist. Jim would tease me and tell me to teach the whole room. So at the sock hops, I'd become the maestro of the Twist.

Back to the Beatles. I didn't get it. Their haircuts, their accents. Furthermore, they always appeared stoned or "spaced out," not that unusual in the music scene, but noticeable to me in my early days of band exposure. I have to say, though, they were pleasant and they enjoyed their ride with fame and fortune—just having a grand old time. The "Fab Four" showed up a couple of times thereafter, in Atlanta and Houston, and we'd end up going to dinner together—Jim, myself, John, George, Ringo, and Paul. I suspect they probably knew that Jim and I were a couple, but it was never addressed or discussed. I don't know if it was discretion or respect to Jim, who was quite powerful in his part of the music world; I marveled at how they so easily interacted with one another. Ringo Starr was my favorite Beatle—probably because he reminded me of Jim. I was usually quiet at these dinners and let Jim do the conversational pivoting.

Then there were the Rolling Stones! We attended so many of their concerts. After the show we all went out drinking and to dinner. I liked Mick Jagger well enough and I remember him being extraordinarily sweet and affable. He was also always incredibly stoned. Jim and I were just drinkers, and never into the drug scene, although we didn't care what other people did. I couldn't relate to that aspect of Mick—nor could I relate to his seemingly universal appeal. To me, he was unattractive. I chuckle inwardly as I note now that I always knew how to spot a fine decorative showpiece, but I was lousy at recognizing rock star charisma. In any event, it was a fun time. Jim and I traveled all over the country. To all intents and purposes we were married—he even gave me a ring to make it official. This, even though we couldn't make it legal and obtain an actual certificate recognized by the state. That would have to wait forty years or so—and not with Jim!

We even adopted a child, in a manner of speaking—GG, our precious black poodle puppy—clearly not the result of a biological miracle, but our "son" nonetheless. We named him GG for "Good Guy,"

after the on-air DJ team at WSGN-AM. He meant the world to us. By the end of that first year living together, GG was the bond that more than anything else sealed our relationship. Being from a wealthy Texas family, Jim was extremely generous, especially if someone needed something.

Jim loved his career. He helped make WSGN one of the leading top-ten stations in the country. When he was on the air, whether radio or TV, he was truly on! He introduced so many rock-and-roll entertainers. When he wasn't doing his daily radio broadcast, he would do the early-morning weather report from his own airplane. With his magnetic personality, Jim was a true superstar.

Time passed. Eventually, Jim got exactly what he wanted. His divorce was final and he became "that" person in my life. He fell deeply in love and promised me the world.

He made good on his promise. He gave me the world—and I loved every moment of it for our five years together. That is until my life changed again and I realized I wanted a different life—one that I created myself. My way.

I grew restless. While I loved the sock hops and enjoyed meeting the bands and fascinating people, I could not help but realize that the relationship between Jim and me was fading, more so for me than for him. He began traveling more and more for work, and I eventually fell into the temptation of indulging in extramarital sex. Back in the day, I could have any man I wanted—and I took full advantage of that appeal. When Jim was away, I'd head for the gay bars and pick up attractive prospects.

The gay bar was a place to drink and socialize with other men who had interests in common. In the early '60s these bars were situated in dark buildings or houses without windows—hidden from the eyes of law enforcement and operated, in many cases, by the mob. There was always great music on the jukebox or from live entertainment. Piano bars were popular, with people sitting or standing around the piano and singing. Successful piano players like Michael Feinstein started their careers playing in gay bars. In the '70s, it was the disco era, with Studio 54 in New York and the Factory in West Hollywood being famous club destinations. Gays love dancing. I always enjoyed gay bars, whether it was meeting other gay men, talking and socializing, drinking, or dining. I spent the greater part of my life at home or away sitting on a bar stool and having a wonderful time. The gay bars are the same no matter where you live or travel.

I'm sure Jim played around as well when he was away; in short, we simply weren't connecting on a crucial level anymore. That kind of apathy leads to deadly boredom and questionable behavior. I wanted to be more than a trophy. For Jim, that was enough. For me, never. I was always looking to the stars—to that next level of challenge and victory. I was itching to discover myself outside the comfort zone Jim had diligently provided. I wanted to escape Jim, to get away from Birmingham, to fly! I was no different from most men in their twenties—I wanted adventure. The looming questions haunted me: Who was I? Where was I going?

In a way, I knew what I wanted to be. The image of my future reality was clear as day.

How would I get there? That part was still a little murky.

Ultimately, I had become super dependent on Jim and the luxurious lifestyle he afforded me. He treated me like a real "queen" and I reigned for five years until I felt worthless, like a possession. That's what bothered me. I had everything a young man could want—except my own identity. I was spoiled in a way that was now arresting my need to fulfill some undefined destiny.

I knew this to be a truism. For even though I worked and made my own money, Jim never allowed me to pay for anything at all. The dependence was enervating and I knew that, to change this dynamic, I was going to have to do something radical, something drastic. Perhaps even something painful to the one I loved.

That's when I decided to make a drastic change in my life. I had arrived at a major turning point.

Either I moved like a cheetah, fast and soon, or I would be forever mired in a lackluster existence and never realize my greater destiny.

❈8❈

Thirteen Pieces of Unmatched Luggage and My Poodle

DOMESTIC WAR WAS about to start.

Nothing was going to stop me.

Several days earlier, Jim had come home from a business trip and declared that he'd been transferred to Dallas, Texas, to another radio station—one more prestigious than the one in Birmingham. They had offered him the position of program director—an excellent situation.

"I've been promoted," he said, smiling, fully expecting my response to be nothing short of meteoric and joyfully explosive. I failed to deliver. He pressed on. "Bernard, you'll go to Dallas, okay? We'll see a realtor about buying a house. Then we can have a real home!" he exclaimed.

I'm not sure what my expression revealed that day, but I'm sure it was not one of all-out happiness. Birmingham had always been my home and I'd never lived anywhere else. I was not sure that I wanted to go to Dallas, just like that. I'd be in the same state as Jim's mercurial and enigmatic mother. As I had told Jim many times before, "Texas isn't big enough for me and your mother!" It would not be a contest between her and me.

So, I just shrugged at the news. Jim immediately sensed I wasn't thrilled with the idea of moving. This news, coupled with our drifting apart on so many levels, didn't mitigate matters much. As generous as Jim could be, he was also controlling. In past months, he would call me into his office and start line-iteming my credit card expenses. I'd be forced to justify every expenditure and he'd never fail to patronize me.

"Bernard, tell me what this purchase was for? Saks? Three hundred dollars? Really?" His tone sounded like what a father might use with a naughty son.

"Well, there was this coat," I would reply like a defensive child, "that I bought for our trip to Chicago" or some other excuse. He'd then nod and move on to the next item, further humiliating me. I had grown resentful at the patronizing. Bad.

Several days later, Jim again brought up the move to Dallas. "When will you be joining me in Texas?"

Without hesitation, I dropped the bomb: "I've thought about it, Jim, and I'm not going. I won't be joining you."

For a long moment, there was silence. No explosion of anger or surprise. Just ... silence.

"My God," he said at last. "What are you talking about?"

His expression said it all—he was shell-shocked, dumbfounded, hurt to the core. Color drained from his face.

"I called our friends in LA and asked if I could stay with them until I get settled," I said quietly.

Jim's up-to-now calm demeanor collapsed into clear heartbreak. "No," he whispered, more to himself than to me. "No ..."

I knew that I was hurting him terribly, but I also knew what had to be done. That rigidity and determination in me told me not to waver on this decision. I had to get out and there was no good way to end this. That's why things end badly—because it's the end. Yet, even with this realization, I felt an odd sense of relief—of release. I needed to spread my wings and flee this golden cage that Jim had so ardently created for me.

Honestly, I was terrified.

I'd never been on my own. First, there was my family. Then, there was Jim. Soon, it would just be me.

In the succeeding days, Jim moped around, clearly devastated. He was also angry with me. He didn't try to dissuade me from my decision, but his disdain was palpable. I chose to ignore it or at least not let it consume me with guilt. I was twenty-four years old, not to mention good looking and talented. I was ready to conquer the world. The world of Beverly Hills, that is.

The last week of June 1968, I had the moving men come and pack my belongings. I took a few personal items and some furniture I had stored in my sister Sarah's basement. Jim's belongings were shipped to Dallas.

The night before the movers came, Jim, our poodle GG, and I were on the floor. Jim was praying I wouldn't leave—praying for some last miracle, a reprieve to his torment—that I would see the light and choose to stay.

Certainly such a reversal of decision was tempting.

Yet, it was impossible.

I'd pushed the nuclear codes into operation and the missile was launched.

The next day, my thirteen pieces of unmatched luggage and my poodle boarded a flight to California.

I had done it.

I had said my goodbyes to one and all.

I was on the move to Beverly Hills.

God help me, I thought. You're a brave and very strong man.

I was. I truly was!

⇥9⇤

Los Angeles—Meet Bernard Puccio

T HE WHEELS OF the plane hit the tarmac hard and I reached for the seat in front of me, holding on as the aircraft initiated its braking sequence. I had arrived, safe and in one piece. I looked out at the Los Angeles airport and marveled at how large it was—a virtual hub to every exotic place on the planet.

Beverly Hills was only a few miles north, my ultimate destination.

Fear crept into my entire being again, but it was commingled with youthful excitement. This was my adventure—my journey of a thousand lights. I quashed my terror and self-fortified my anxiety with quiet affirmations. I had a few hundred dollars, thirteen pieces of unmatched luggage, and boundless confidence. Who or what could stop me? No one and nothing!

When you're young, it's kind of strange—you allow yourself courage to dream. You have some inalienable giggles about what you dare, but when you're twenty-four, you're a rock god, an unstoppable force of nature. From childhood to the onset of puberty, not many important changes occur in the "male" body. Bones grow, cells divide, and teeth grow in and fall out and grow in again. The pre-puberty male body can take an amazing amount of physical punishment. Young males act as though they are indestructible.

One can see where this sense of omnipotence and imperviousness to damage is a desirable evolutionary setup for the years to come. In order for a male to want to leave the safety of his cave (in my case, Jim's sanctuary) and battle a saber-toothed tiger (fly to Beverly Hills), he would have to believe that he was virtually unstoppable. Only if he has had years of conditioning to reinforce this belief would he willingly pick up the sharp stick and go kill the beast. So the pre-puberty years are the training ground, the time in a male's life where his body forgives almost every sort of punishment, and heals amazingly quickly.

Once puberty hits, powerful hormones coursing through his system amplify the sense of invulnerability. He is likely to believe he is invincible, and his body sends him signals that indeed he is. Again, from an evolutionary standpoint, what you would want in young males is an almost foolhardy conviction that nothing can go wrong and that they will always persevere. Even in modern times, this aggressive overestimation of the male's power is what military forces depend upon. You don't see many forty-year-olds signing up to get shot at, but recruiting stations are filled with eighteen-year-olds who want to see the world through the lens of a sniper scope.

My point being—by way of young male analysis—that I was a superhero in my own mind and I was here to vanquish Gotham City, or in my case, Beverly Hills. I was here to kick butt, poodle and all!

That being said, the first four days of my new life in Los Angeles were hard. I had to get used to being on my own. I started looking for work immediately and knew exactly where I wished to obtain employment. I found a living situation with friends at the former estate of silent screen star Norma Talmadge in the Hollywood Hills.

One of them took me downtown to Robinson's—a well-known department store at the time.

I entered the design studio of the store and met with a pleasant woman, the ostensible director. She perused my design portfolio thoughtfully. I was, of course, dressed for the interview. The lady politely declined my offerings.

"I'm sorry. There's no opening at this time," she said. "If you leave your number, I will contact you when something becomes available." I complied, then immediately went to Barker Bros, a furniture company down the street, and was hired on the spot. The word *no* was not really part of my life lexicon—I didn't do well with rejection.

One weekend, I took a mini-trip to San Francisco. I had met a man there when I was with Jim and we had had a torrid affair. Sex with Jim had become pedestrian and dull—I was cutting loose. Not only with the San Fran man, but with guys right and left.

I returned to Los Angeles and to my new job at Barker Bros. Two weeks later I received a call from the director at Robinson's Design Studio. The decision had been reversed and the store now wished to hire me. I was literally blown away. This was it! This was the true beginning of my interior design career.

I was on my way—exactly as I had visualized it!

Robinson's—here I come!

⇥10⇤
Beverly Hills—
Meet Bernard-o!

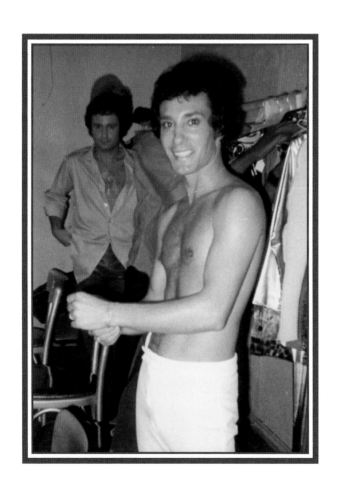

T HE DIE HAD been cast.

I now seemed headed toward a future of uncertain success. In my mind, it was the perfect direction, just as I had planned all along.

Robinson's Department Store hired me as one of four interior designers. Our team was composed of two men and two women and our assignments, respectively, were to enhance the model apartments for a new condominium development complex. This was no small undertaking as the thirty-two-story Bunker Hill Tower was rather large, consisting of 256 units, and occupied a prominent position in the Bunker Hill neighborhood in downtown Los Angeles, once home to Victorian houses that were either demolished or relocated.

Each one of us had the opportunity to design the interior of one model apartment. This was a dream come true for me! I was now creating and beautifying autonomously with creative license. I, of course, endeavored to make my interior the most fabulous of the four. My competitive nature would not be outdone on this mission. I pursued my dream of coming out No. 1.

After surveying the space I was assigned, it took me two weeks to put together the floor plans, furniture layout, colors, fabrics, and wall finishes. Everything was new. I was working with a clean slate. Since it was a high-rise building, there were beautiful views of downtown Los Angeles.

I decided to create a contemporary design using a color scheme consisting of beige, off-white, a touch of red, and my signature black accents. It was an eclectic look—extremely comfortable for either a man or woman or a couple. This was a model apartment and I wanted to appeal to everyone's taste and style. I always introduce color in the artwork, be it with accent pillows, fresh flowers, or accessories—personal touches that make for a homey environment.

I searched the whole city. Most people favored traditional design at the time, inspired by European décor, elegant, yet comfortable.

Although I could accomplish any style, my preferred look was "eclectic." That was my claim to fame, mixing time periods, old and new, textures and colors, but you must know how to accomplish it.

My model condo received distinguished reviews in the *Los Angeles Times* Home Section. From that point on, I was off—or, to put it another way, I had arrived! This write-up was instrumental in obtaining a clientele of worth and volume that desired the Puccio touch for their own residences in Bunker Hill. My career was suddenly "happening." Happy and proud, I was truly on the right path as a verifiable talent to be reckoned with.

I thought life couldn't get better than this.

I was wrong.

After designing a few other Bunker Hill condos, in short order, I was referred to one particular client who was so moved by what I had designed that she asked if she could "tip" me for a job well done. She was a charming elderly lady with lots of money. She loved the eclectic décor of my model and gave me carte blanche to design her residence. I delivered what she wanted and more.

Tips were not exactly customary, but she was so enthusiastic at what I had accomplished, I figured it would be downright rude for me not to accept a small gratuity for my efforts. This particular client was wealthy beyond words and her tip was not unappreciated. What is more important, it drove me forward psychologically to exceed my expectations.

Thus, I received a $500 gift check.

The year was 1969; I remember it well. This was not chump change back in the day. I was so delighted that I had my furniture shipped out from Birmingham to Los Angeles shortly thereafter and acquired my first apartment, all within a matter of days. It was an exhilarating time indeed!

Another component of this success was I moved past Jim and our time together as a "couple." I was independent now. I was content to still speak with him from time to time, but I became naturally less involved emotionally with that remembrance as my life in Los Angeles continued to accelerate.

Jim was not going to let go that easily; he continued to push and push through communication, hoping to change my mind about remaining in LA. In this effort, he was doomed to failure. I was now dating some ultra-cool men. Happy and independent, I was sexually explorative on my own terms. Los Angeles was my home now. I was no longer anyone's trophy, no one's chattel, and no one's husband. I would never be able to go back to what was.

I liked Los Angeles, and especially Beverly Hills.

In turn, Beverly Hills really liked me.

Before I moved into my new digs, I had shared a small apartment with a guy named Taylor in Studio City. Taylor was a young, gay fellow I had met in a bar one night and we had become fast friends. He had recently returned from being on tour with The Young Americans and Johnny Mathis, and he was a very agreeable guy but financially strapped. Of course, when I moved in with him, I fixed up the place with style just to make it livable. As he lived in a one-bedroom, I was relegated to a sofa in the living room.

Taylor was in constant job-hunt mode. The interviews he went on weekly were numerous. One day, he came home and announced that he had had an interview with Lana Turner. He could barely contain his excitement. I must admit, butterflies flapped in my belly as well at the mention of her name. I adored this beautiful movie star. I thought somewhat wryly about how my life had progressed to this point. I had pretended once to walk like her and act like her, and here I was—one degree of separation from the real thing.

I was, of course, delighted for Taylor as he talked about the interview.

"She wants me to be her personal assistant. Well, if I get the job, that is. It would be perfect." I nodded in concurrence.

Later that evening, Taylor announced he was heading out but

begged me to stay close to the phone in case Lana Turner happened to call. As luck would have it, I had nothing planned that evening and agreed to his request.

The phone rang around 9:30 p.m.

I answered it and a woman's voice lilted across the line. "Hello, may I speak to Taylor?"

"I'm sorry, he's out for the evening. May I take a message?"

"Who's this?" the sweet lady voice questioned.

"I'm Bernard, Taylor's roommate."

A momentary beat, then: "Darling, I'm Lana Turner."

I damn near fainted on the spot, but was saved this lapse of consciousness as Lana suddenly began choking from her end of the phone.

I waited a few seconds, allowing her to regain some vocal composure. The choking continued.

"Ms. Turner, please put down the phone and get some water," I said sincerely. I waited. Silence. Then:

"Oh, darling, thank you," she said, sincerely grateful.

It was a pinch-me moment. Here I was helping Lana Turner through a mild choking event.

"Bernard, Taylor mentioned you to me at his interview. I'd like to hire him as my personal secretary. Would you let him know, please?"

"Yes, I'll do that, Ms. Turner," I said.

"Thank you, dear," she replied.

"Ms. Turner, I know Taylor will be ecstatic. I know he really wanted the job."

"I look forward to meeting you, Bernard," she said.

I couldn't help myself and pressed forward. "Ms. Turner, you can't imagine how thrilled I am to talk with you. I've adored all of your movies."

"Why, thank you, Bernard. Good night," she said.

I had no idea then how Lana Turner would figure so prominently in my life thereafter.

It struck me how sublimely surreal the conversation had been. Here I was, in Los Angeles, having traveled here with my thirteen pieces of unmatched luggage and my poodle, and now having spoken with Lana Turner. It was a shock to both my psyche and my soul, but in a good way. All of this happened in a matter of three months.

Taylor, of course, was thrilled with the news. At least initially—poor Taylor had no idea how his association with Lana Turner would affect his life. He later became jealous of my bond with Lana. I didn't work for her, but we happened to become close friends. Years later, Lana and Taylor's relationship would come to a turbulent end. That evening at least was one of pure joy for him.

Residing with Taylor in a one-bedroom apartment was short-lived—less than a year. It was uncomfortable for us both. I was anxious to get my own place and have my personal belongings shipped from Alabama. I decided to stay in Los Angeles and start a new life. Work was going great at Robinson's and I had closed all bonds with Jim in Texas. That's when I moved into my first apartment in Beverly Hills—just GG and me! I was living alone now for the first time and I liked it!

In the succeeding weeks, I met a tall, good-looking fellow named Steve, a singer from New York who had, like me, come out to LA to strike it rich. He was handsome, to be sure, but didn't have two nickels to rub together. He wanted to move in with me and I simply couldn't say no. We lasted about a year until I discovered Steve was a habitual drug addict—or at the very least had a grand capacity to abuse any number of chemicals to great personal detriment.

I try not to judge anyone too harshly. You realize as you get older that almost everyone is fucked up to some degree or another. That being said, I really wasn't interested in pursuing this relationship. I was seeking the right man for me while I was also having sex with every hot guy in town. Yes, having my cake and eating it, too!

I dated young men, older men, successful men, and incredibly wealthy men who introduced me to the crème de la crème of Los Angeles. If you're good looking, you've got carte blanche to run the town according to your own precepts. As I was both hot and well spoken, I fit in beautifully. In time, I met all the influential gay people in town with their beautiful homes, cars, jewelry, and parties. Being the new kid on the block, I was accepted by one and all.

I had Beverly Hills in the palm of my hand.

It, in turn, had me as well.

No complaints.

It was the best of the best with beneficial collaboration.

❧ 11 ❧

"Who Loves You Baby?"

Beverly Hills—1969

I WAS STILL AT Robinson's in the year they put a man on the moon and I was doing quite well for myself. The company had fired their primary designer at the Beverly Hills store and asked me if I had interest in moving uptown, as it were. I jumped at the opportunity to work at the most distinguished department store in the city. This was a definite step up and exactly where I had wanted to be since day one. Beverly Hills was exactly where I wanted to work.

The job was more than prestigious—it was royal in nature. Beverly Hills was a positive adjustment from downtown LA. It was posh and tip-top throughout. I dovetailed into this society seamlessly, playing my part well as "designer to the stars." Robinson's at this time was home to the carriage trade. Rolls-Royces and limos would regularly pull out in front of the main doors and God knows who might step out, be they stars or royalty.

My first big design project was for actor Telly Savalas, who was, back in the day, arguably one of the top TV stars around. He played Kojak in the long-running series of the same name. He was Greek, flamboyant, and known for his panache and his perennial lollipop sucking—an apparent prop to the character he played weekly to an audience of millions.

"Who loves ya, baby?" was Kojak's branded wisecracking quip after solving almost every case as one of New York's top detectives. Telly was a bigger-than-life character in the real world, too. I came to know his family quite well and in time was made to feel part of the Savalas family. As per Greek reputation, the family was a huge, joyful tribe that liked to do everything in largesse, from parties to home life. They were lovely people.

I designed the Savalas French Regency home on Whittier Drive in Beverly Hills, which formerly belonged to Paul Newman and Joanne Woodward—whom I got to meet before the Savalases moved in. The Newmans had painted all the rooms in the main house in dark colors. Telly's wife, Lynn, requested we go light. I gave the home a complete makeover. In keeping with the home's architectural style, I selected elegant French furniture using beautiful imported silk fabrics.

Telly, Lynn, and their two adorable daughters lived in the large house, while his mother, Christina, occupied the guesthouse. I felt a special affection for Christina. She was a fascinating woman, an amazing artist, and a former Miss Greece, decades earlier. Her art had a kind of Picasso quality that was quite exceptional. We became quite close.

The Savalases were a lovely, easygoing family. Upon completion of their project, and in appreciation of my work, Telly gave me a personalized autographed photo and a complete stereo sound system. My favorite gift, which I still possess, is an original piece of art from Christina Savalas.

I worked for Telly and his family for five years. Through him, I met a number of celebrities, like Sidney Poitier and famed restaurateur Steve Crane.

My career was going great! I loved working as an interior designer at Robinson's Beverly Hills. I was in my late twenties and eager to learn.

This position offered me the opportunity to meet many celebrities. Everyone shopped at this store. It was before Neiman Marcus opened.

This particular day I was at my desk. I looked up and saw this very tall man with several packages in hand. He looked like he needed help. As I approached, he turned around and I realized it was Rock Hudson. I will never forget that moment as long as I live. He looked down at me. He was six feet five and I was five feet six! I asked if he needed help.

"I would love some help to my car," he replied in an extraordinarily deep voice.

"I'll call for assistance," I said.

I left to make the phone call. I became so nervous. I had just met Rock Hudson. Wow! I will never forget his eyes meeting mine. I felt faint. I had never experienced that feeling before—and I never felt it again. When I returned to tell Mr. Hudson help was on the way, we began to talk. He asked me who I was and my position. I explained I was head interior designer for Robinson's.

After a few minutes and many questions, a store assistant arrived to help Rock to his car with his purchases. It was the Christmas holiday. I personally escorted Mr. Hudson to his car. That's when he reached down and shook my hand to thank me. I said what a great pleasure it was to meet him. I had seen all his movies, and especially loved *Giant* with Elizabeth Taylor. He smiled and said he loved working with her. They were great friends. Then he asked if I had time to have coffee or a drink with him.

I looked at his incredibly handsome face and admitted truthfully, "I would love to, but I have to get back to my office."

He thanked me for helping him and said, "Hopefully we'll meet again." I walked away feeling giddy as a kid—so excited to have met Rock Hudson.

Returning to my office, I was in shock at what had just transpired. I could not believe I said no to his offer. I have always wondered how my life would have possibly changed had I gone out with him.

Years later, I would work with his close friend Elizabeth Taylor designing and coordinating the first Commitment to Life benefit, raising money for AIDS research while, at the same time, Rock was in a Paris hospital dying from the virus. After getting to know Elizabeth Taylor, I felt I could tell her about Rock Hudson. She smiled with joy and said she just adored him. I will never forget meeting two of my favorite movie icons.

I met many celebrities and influential people in the ensuing years. One day the president of Robinson's called me to his office and asked if I would pay a visit to Virginia Robinson's home in Beverly Hills to assist her in some decorating. She was the widow of Harry Winchester Robinson, the heir to J.W. Robinson's Department Store. I was so honored. I arrived at the stately 1911 gated estate, one of the first homes to be built in Beverly Hills just above Sunset Boulevard, and later to become a historical landmark famed for its botanical gardens which were exceptionally beautiful—some terraced and containing magnolia and citrus trees. There were floral gardens, palm trees, and cypress flanking extensive green lawns.

I was introduced to Mrs. Robinson, a dignified lady with white hair, seated on a chaise lounge with her dogs. She adored her beautiful pets. Our meeting was in the early seventies and I enjoyed designing and giving her residence a new look, not at all pretentious. I added colorful print fabrics and solids to create a garden effect on the window treatments and furniture. She was extremely happy. Mrs. Robinson was a lovely and charming lady. After her passing, her home and gardens were turned over to the County of Los Angeles, open for tours and charitable events. I've had the great pleasure of going to the Virginia Robinson Gardens for special events. Years later, I could still see some of my decorating. It was old, but still looked lovely and comfortable. That's the look that Virginia Robinson wanted and I accomplished.

While at Robinson's, I also got to meet Max Steiner, the great composer of hundreds of famous film scores like *Gone with the Wind*, *Casablanca*, and *King Kong*.

When I arrived at his home, the butler showed me to the music studio. Mr. Steiner was sitting at the piano. After our introduction, realizing he had an ardent fan, Mr. Steiner asked if he could play something for me. I said I would love it. Upon finishing two beautiful compositions, Mr. Steiner motioned to his butler, who then helped him stand up. It was then I realized he was blind. It certainly didn't affect his ability to play.

Mr. Steiner said he would like to show me around the house. He requested I only change the fabrics I perceived were worn. During the next few weeks, I made the necessary changes, keeping, at his request, every piece of furniture in the exact same place. He felt the fabric choices, which helped make his decisions, while I guided the color selections. These changes were strictly for comfort. It was a pleasure to work with him. Every time I see his name in the credits of a film, I remember that special afternoon.

One day I was in my design studio. The phone rang and a woman asked whether Robinson's had a pink velvet sofa. I said no, but I could certainly order one. A few hours later I looked up from my desk to see a beautiful young woman with her young son. Turns out it was the lady inquiring about the pink velvet sofa, Mrs. Steve Crane, whose husband had been married to Lana Turner.

By this time, I had become rather close with Lana and was about to become Leslie Crane's best friend for years to come. Steve owned many of the finest restaurants in Beverly Hills and other places as well—Stefaninos, Au Petit Jean, and the iconic Luau were but a few of Steve's dining establishments.

The Luau was a wonderful hangout, especially for hookers. The maître d' was Joe Stellini, a handsome Italian and a good friend. Leslie and I were roughly the same age while Steve was twenty-eight years older than us both. She was young and fun and it was a fine feeling to know that my company made her so happy. We began to frequent clubs and parties together. I was introduced through her to the inside circle of Beverly Hills and, as my reputation as a designer increased, so too did my partying. I was known as a guy who worked hard by day and partied like an animal by night. I liked the rep enormously and it was a deserved one at that.

Steve's daughter with Lana, Cheryl Crane, was also an acquaintance, though we had an uneasy friendship. This was mainly because Leslie was smoking hot, younger, and married to Cheryl's father. I was soon immersed, by way of my relationship with Lana, in a rather fractious family dynamic that treaded a fine line of stability.

Notwithstanding this somewhat uneasy family alliance, Steve adored me. He knew I was gay, didn't care, and loved the idea of my escorting his wife, Leslie, to events on a regular basis. This freed Steve up to play cards and otherwise gamble the night away with his guy friends.

He soon took to calling my office to request that I accompany Leslie out to whatever event she might wish to attend. He would send a limo for us and, of course, everything was carte blanche.

The 1970 Thalians Ball, my first black-tie charity event hosted by Debbie Reynolds and Ruta Lee, was a highlight. The Mr. Wonderful honoree that year was television toastmaster Ed Sullivan. Singer Tom Jones was the headliner. It was a grand evening. I got to meet or see many celebrities who would later become friends and attend my events.

Leslie enjoyed going to Pip's, a private membership club founded by Hugh Hefner, to dance and play backgammon, the current game rage in the disco era. We also enjoyed the vibe at The Factory, an exclusive nightclub with live entertainment, later to become the popular gay club Studio One.

A night out would not be complete without a stop for dinner and drinks at one of Steve Crane's popular Beverly Hills restaurants, and of course we made the rounds of the gay bars. Leslie liked to smoke grass, while I preferred cocktails. She was beautiful and we looked divine together. My friends loved Leslie and went crazy over Lana Turner.

This exciting routine went on for years.

I never questioned my good fortune or the peculiarities of the family Crane dynamic, which, of course, prominently included Lana, like it or not. For me, seeing both Lana Turner and Leslie was like tiptoeing through a potential minefield, which fortunately never really exploded, at least not for me.

Anyway, all their drama affected me only peripherally; generally, it was nights out with either Leslie or Lana, followed by tight-jean-outfitted me heading off to the gay bars for some serious and assiduous sex.

It was a euphoric time for me.

Leslie Crane

❧12❧
Lana Turner—Movie Star

Lana Turner

TWO YEARS AFTER I'd moved to Los Angeles, Jim and I were more than finished. I'd cut off all ties. I would never forget him—my first lover from Alabama—but now he was a distant memory.

I was now living in a different world, occupying a different plane of existence.

Taylor had introduced me to Lana Turner and we took to one another immediately. Our first meeting ended with Lana kissing me on the cheek. It doesn't get much better than that. Come on—she'd been my childhood idol. I was helpless. We exchanged numbers and she began calling me to go out regularly. Taylor was none too thrilled about this, but I could give a damn.

In the ensuing years, Lana and I became more than acquaintances—we became a virtual team. Her entourage included her hairstylist and Taylor. They weren't crazy about our relationship, but that disapproval stemmed mainly from jealousy.

We had a ball together. She adored me for who I was—a creature of style, individuality, good looks, and panache. She liked my sense of fun. We were also astoundingly compatible drinking buddies, able to go toe-to-toe with one another in the boozing arena. I believe it was with Lana where my drinking went from moderate to heavy. Still, I know her affection for me was not based on drinking. I was merely her pal and she liked that immensely.

She knew, of course, that I was gay and had no interest in having sex with women. I wasn't aspiring to be an actor. I wanted nothing from her. I loved Lana solely for her unique spirit, plain and simple.

The press soon took notice of our relationship, as our public exposure had transcended itself into the realm of local fame. If we went out together to an event, it would be mentioned thus: "Lana and her Italian designer friend were out on the town again." Words to that effect. We loved going to films together. Often, we'd attire ourselves in large coats and sunglasses to ward off excessive press attention, always failed endeavors on our part to attempt anonymity. Most of the time, the clever press would uncover her. This was Lana's life and it thus became mine.

Lana and I essentially had become an item, albeit a platonic one. That was going to change soon in a very bizarre and surreal way.

It was Monday night—the Academy Awards.

From the beginning of our friendship, we had always watched the Oscars together. On this particular Monday, in this particular year, she had invited me along with Taylor and a couple of friends from Palm Springs to watch the awards show. Lana didn't like crowds in her apartment. She always ordered food in from The Luau and we would end up sitting around, eating and drinking, watching the show. Lana loved to drink vodka—and plenty of it. We all consumed enough Stoli to choke a small SEAL platoon. It was a blast.

The drunker Lana got, the more she transformed herself into a kind of little-girl mode, replete with a little-girl voice that was oddly grating. I called it "baby talk" and with good reason. She would then take to calling me "darling" at the beginning of almost every sentence. She had also blessed me with a new Latinized name, which everyone soon picked up.

I had, thanks to Lana, now become . . . Bernardo!

"Bernardo, darling, one more drink?"

"Bernardo, darling, pour me another, won't you?"

"Bernardo, darling . . ."

On and on.

Though in her fifties, Lana Turner retained a supernatural beauty. She lived modestly, compared to most movie stars. Instead of some mansion in Beverly Hills or Malibu, she occupied a condo in Century City on the eighteenth floor. She would die there. She was the real deal as a movie star, created by the studio system, marketed and packaged by a dynasty of filmmakers who sold her to the masses like toilet paper.

Even so, she was an enigma. Solitary and independent, Lana Turner was a true star and she had lived an adventurous lifestyle, traveling the world with her staff, friends, and adoring fans. This was all she really desired. She had achieved all of her dreams and then some.

After five years, our relationship had become, in a word, strange. Odd episodes of late haunted me mildly. One time, Lana showed up at my apartment in a fur coat, invited herself in, then dropped the coat to the floor, revealing herself to be wearing a black workout jumpsuit. She wanted to exercise and wanted me to join her, which I did.

Other moments of weirdness occurred, but they were not singularly disturbing; they were more disconcerting collectively, and on this particular Monday night they would all converge explosively—and I mean that literally.

The Academy Awards had finished and Lana's guests were all preparing to leave. I, too, was ready to exit the festivities—work loomed large for me at the beginning of the week and I was more than feeling the effects of the large amounts of alcohol I had consumed earlier in the evening.

As I was about to put on my jacket, Lana reached for me. "Darling, please don't go. Bernardo, stay and drink with me awhile longer," she begged in that infuriating baby-talk voice of hers.

I complied. Reluctantly.

It was past midnight. Carmen, Lana's housekeeper, had long ago departed for her room, shortly after the guests left. It was just Lana and me.

The moment came when I knew it would be best to leave. Now. Immediately.

"I think I have to go, Lana," I said—or slurred. Can't quite remember.

"My darling, stay. One last drink."

Against my better judgment, I stayed.

"Bernardo, darling, you know how much I love you. Don't you?"

She was getting sloppy and my patience factor was diminishing, especially with the baby talk.

"You're such a great friend to me, Bernardo, darling," she whimpered. "You love me for me. You do. You love me for me, Bernardo."

I nodded wearily, doing my best to maintain a contented smile.

Time took on a surreal transition, my Catholic education kicking in at the weirdest moments. Suddenly Lana and I were kissing. Then we were clutching on to one another like the last remaining survivors on the *Titanic*. I thought to myself: I'm here making out with Lana Turner. I knew she was a friend and that the alcohol compromised her. I also knew that I was feeling severe discomfort at what was transpiring—and at what would inevitably transpire, if I allowed this course of activity to continue. I was immobilized by anxiety, not wanting to hurt or do anything injurious emotionally or mentally to Lana, who was blitzed at the moment.

Not only that, but my mind oddly flitted to the stabbing of underworld figure Johnny Stompanato, Lana's lover, many years before. It was one of those bizarre murders committed by Lana's then fourteen-year-old daughter, Cheryl. Rumors had flown for months after the crime and were still ongoing years later. Was it the young daughter who killed Johnny ... or Lana herself? Could Cheryl really have committed this violent crime or was I currently embracing a homicidal murderer of some distinct fame and irrefutable beauty?

Don't ask me why, but it was during this cross-lateral mental trip that I noticed, to my shock and dismay, I had a hard-on.

Lana continued her inappropriate seduction. She unzipped my trousers, with a certain amount of drunken abandon, which I chose to ignore in the heat of the moment. When she took me into her mouth, I felt an instant sense of violation, of helplessness ... and it was one of the most humiliating sensations I had experienced to date. Inside my addled, sex-induced consciousness of the moment, I was trying to find a rational logic to this insanity. After all, I was a gay man with zero interest in women on a sexual level, yet why this sense of arousal?

After I climaxed, no words were exchanged, no pleasantries, no post-coital superficialities or expressions of once-in-a-lifetime awe. No, it was an exercise in transitory and suppressed hysteria, which to this day I little understand, but it changed our relationship forever. I kissed Lana goodnight and left in shock and embarrassment. This was my first and only sexual experience with a woman.

We are such stuff as dreams are made of, as the Bard echoed in one of those dreary plays. In a way, I was a pivotal and crucial dream for the iconic Lana Turner that night. I was an actor fulfilling a critical role in her needed angst for perpetual love and adoration. I had performed, not as a victim, but as a cherished friend. I feel no regret today, only a profound emptiness that's difficult to comprehend.

We are all too easily hurt.

After that night, my friendship with Lana definitely changed. I felt different, maybe even dirty—perplexed by my sexual dishonesty and repulsed by my lack of self-control. I divorced myself from the world for a while. I instead decided to occupy an inner circle of gay men.

In truth, I had enjoyed that moment of sexual pleasure—and won't ever forget it!

I had had sex with Lana Turner and physically liked it.

So where was I to go from there? I wondered more than twice.

Was I even still gay? What a strange thought.

I had no desire for this to happen. But I think for Lana it was like a challenge. She truly cared for me, but unfortunately, I did not feel for her in a sexual way. I didn't talk to Lana for a long time, although I still cared for her. The sexual encounter had destroyed our friendship, and what we had enjoyed in the past had now evaporated into the veils and mists of time and disenchantment.

I threw myself into work, determined to "recover" from the Lana experience, refusing to be destroyed psychologically.

Yet I could not help but wonder, after that strange Monday night, had I taken to my breast, in lust and drunken friendship, not a beautiful movie star but, rather, a calculating, predatory murderer who may or may not have killed Johnny Stompanato?

The question haunts me still.

There is no relief to be enjoyed on this matter.

There never will be.

❧ 13 ❧

My World Expands

Bernardo—MY NEW NAME now and forever. I liked the alteration, no matter its genesis—the brainchild from my Lana Turner experience. It had a certain remindful resonance which I rather enjoyed—and was not unbecoming a notable interior designer like myself.

I was still well situated at Robinson's in Beverly Hills. By the early '70s, I was making more than just a good living. Many people considered me to be very successful. I was dating more good-looking men and had taken on some fabulous lovers. Young, smart, and in demand, I was truly enjoying my life, working all day and meeting fascinating celebrities, actors, writers, producers, and a panoply of other intriguing luminaries by night. In the design world, socializing and work went hand in hand.

I had very little in the way of competition, or, if I did have some, I was unaware of it. New designers came and ultimately quickly vanished. I was a superstar at what I did. I did not know how long it would last, nor did I care. I was in the present and reveling in the ride.

One of my friends in the design world was Bob Myers, a very

successful interior designer. He took me under his wings and introduced me to everyone, and I mean everyone, who was important in the design world. Bob became a close friend and a great teacher. I always appreciated our friendship as well as the one with his partner, Tony Tonon. I have great memories of our wonderful years together. Bob always said I would take over the design world of Beverly Hills. Years later, he would say to me, "Bernardo, I told you the first day we met, you had what it takes to be a superstar designer." I cherished our long friendship and never forgot what he said to me.

Bob was the one who invited me to my first Beverly Hills "gay party." It was in the summer of 1970, and at the time I didn't know that I would become his protégé. On that Sunday afternoon in July, I drove to Bob's home. After greetings, Bob showed me around his beautiful home. So decorated! It was very theatrical and so Bob. I was truly impressed. After the tour, Bob suggested we go out to the pool and get a drink, something I really needed after the museum tour. Bob said, "I want you to meet Scotty, my bartender." I think that was one of the most memorable and shocking moments of my life. What Bob forgot to mention was that this good-looking, masculine guy was mixing drinks while completely nude with his ten-inch cock. What a shock! I did not know at the time that Scotty would become a dear friend who worked for me for over forty-five years as bartender at my parties, but never in the raw.

Scotty's claim to fame, later to be explored in a best-selling book and film, was that he had been a pimp for the old guard of Hollywood stars, satisfying both sexes with everything they desired. I never met anyone like Scotty!

One day, I received an unexpected visit from someone I never would have expected. My assistant pulled me aside and said, "You have a call from a Mrs. Taber."

My first thought was typically Puccio melodramatic—Jim had died. I had heard through the grapevine that, after he moved to El

Paso and bought his own radio station, he wasn't faring too well. I was never clear on the definition of "not faring too well"—was it drug abuse, depression, or disease? I simply didn't know.

I thanked my assistant, closed my office door, and picked up the phone.

"Hello, Mrs. Taber," I said neutrally.

I couldn't imagine for the life of me why she was calling. She and her husband had never accepted that Jim and I were a couple, and, to be frank, as I have already stated, I was no great fan of this woman.

"Hi, Bernard," she said. "I'm glad I caught you. I'm in town and I thought it might be lovely to see you if you have some time today."

At first, in an almost irrational adolescent brush with momentary fury, I wanted to tell her to fuck off. I restrained myself and sighed. "Sure. Let's meet at the Brown Derby in Beverly Hills. Two p.m.?"

"Fine," she said warmly and hung up the phone.

I showed up exactly at 2:00 p.m. and so did she. I greeted her warmly (spoiler alert—I should have won the Academy Award for that hug).

Mrs. Taber had not changed a bit. Our exchange, even preliminary, was as tense as ever. We sat down at last and commented on the weather. Then she got to the point of her visit.

"Bernard," she began, "I know for years my husband and I never accepted you. I'm sorry for that. My son loved you very much!" She emphasized the final words.

"How is Jim?" I asked, sincerely curious.

"Not well, I'm afraid. I need you to get back together with him," she answered. Her voice sounded weak and deflated. Defeated. "I'm afraid if you don't, he's going to die."

I stared blankly at her, my mind awash of frenetic images of Jim collapsing, myself sobbing. Her plea had caught me off guard. Mable Taber then took out a single check, folded in half, and pushed it slowly across the table.

This woman had offered me a signed blank check—a bribe, or a plea—to return to Dallas to her desperate son, my one-time lover.

I pushed the check back, gently, and looked her square in the eye. "Mable, I will never get back together with your son. He gave me an incredible life and taught me so much about myself, but I'm now able to be on my own and be the man I always wished to be. I will always be appreciative for all he did. As much as I loved him, I need my independence."

I stood up, said my "goodbyes," and left the restaurant.

That was the last time I ever spoke with any of the Tabers. Many years later I learned that Jim had struggled with addiction and had passed away at fifty-two years of age from brain cancer. When I heard of his death, I was traumatized even after such duration of time and absence. He had been extremely generous to me and I'll always remember Jim Taber as a good man whom I loved very much. And he adored me!

In the subsequent years following my fateful meeting with Mable Taber, I ran around in various circles of gay men of all ages from varied backgrounds and different careers. This was all post–Lana Turner. I had to some degree survived that psychological onslaught and was for a time living it up.

It seems like the '70s were truly some of the most memorable and definitely the sexiest years of my life. This was before AIDS.

I flew to New York City at least once a year. I loved checking out Bloomingdale's room settings, seeing theater, and enjoying this fabulous city. For one such trip, I met up with my best friend Bill Clutter. He was living in Washington, DC, at the time and we were planning a few crazy days together in NYC.

Bill is and always will be a great fun person to be with. Always positive, Bill loved to drink as much as I did. We were staying at the United Nations Plaza Hotel, and our friend Tommy Christopher was also in town and joining us for dinner this particular night. We were dining at this exclusive elegant restaurant—The Leopard.

After dinner we decided to go bar hopping. I told Bill I wanted to go back to our hotel to change into more suitable, less dressy clothes. After all we were in suits. So back we went to our hotel. Bill went into the bathroom first and it never takes him long. Then I went into the bathroom to change. Of course it takes me longer.

We were staying on the seventeenth floor of the hotel. This was an older New York hotel with two small windows that opened only slightly for safety reasons. Hot water was dripping into the bathtub. I forgot to mention, it was pouring rain outside. The combination of hot water from the tub and the rain outside created a lot of moisture while I was changing and freshening up. I opened the window. The bathroom interior was getting very steamy. Then I heard Bill say, "Bernardo, Tommy and I are going to the bar. We will meet you there."

I thought, Great. I don't have to hurry. I proceeded to finish my grooming. Then I tried to open the door. It would not open. I tried again and again. No luck. After a few minutes, I began to panic. I have terrible claustrophobia. I began to scream and bang on the door. No one could hear me. The hot water dripping and the rain outside had turned the room into a sauna. I began screaming out of the small window, which opened enough to get my arm out. I took a white towel and started waving it out of the window, continuing to scream for help. This went on for over an hour. Finally, the hotel sent security up to break the bathroom door open and rescue me. I was a complete wreck and furious. I went down to the lobby. That's when the hotel clerk told me someone saw me waving for help and called the front desk. No sign of Bill or Tommy. I left the hotel, sat on the curb in the rain, and cried. I just wanted out of the bathroom.

Later that night when Bill and Tommy returned, very late and drunk, I told them what happened. They became hysterical. I was furious that they didn't wait for me. I have had many bad experiences with getting stuck in bathrooms with broken locks.

I was spending most of my leisure time at an extremely popular gay club called the Garden District on La Cienega Boulevard in what is now West Hollywood. My routine there consisted primarily of drinking, socializing, and wild times best left to the imagination versus being documented here for posterity. This was gay headquarters—where everything and everyone was happening.

By way of a little history, the Garden District was named after a New Orleans neighborhood—the birthplace of the club's owner, Nicky Nichols. Open for lunch and dinner, the Garden District was a windowless, low-lit, intimate dining room with red leather booths adjacent to a bustling bar scene. Indoor trees with white accent lights helped create a garden atmosphere. The men's room was labeled Thorns and the women's room Roses.

I remember listening to Glen Campbell's No. 1 single "Southern Nights" being played on the jukebox. After a couple of drinks, my friends and I would get up and dance. Everything was relatively inexpensive. One could live it up on a fraction of what things cost today. The menu featured the best southern fried chicken and shrimp.

I was "Queen B" of this joint, and if I had a buck for every trick I picked up there, I'd be a rich man today. I must emphasize, this sexual behavior was all pre-AIDS, so fear was a stranger to the gay community, an alien simply not present in the cultural climate of homosexual behavior.

I became close friends with one of the bartenders. His nickname was Frieda. He was a brilliant, smart, and witty guy. I found out he was also MC for a big Halloween costume ball I had attended for years called the GGRC, short for Gay Girls Riding Club, held at a hotel near the LA airport. Hundreds of guys would come from all over for this annual event. These "queens" would work on their costumes for a year with hopes of outdoing the competition and winning the Best Prize trophy. I decided to attend the ball—of course in costume. That year the theme was *Parade*. Frieda gave me all the info, and I decided to put together an Easter Parade group. I always adored that special holiday with all the beautiful clothes and elaborate hats, of course. So I let my imagination go to work. A few days later I was sitting at the Garden District bar when four of my friends walked in. I asked if they would be interested in participating at the GGRC Ball in costumes. To my surprise they said yes and asked, "What is it?" I explained it was a drag ball and I had decided to enter as an Easter Parade group. They said, "Let's go for it! Let's win first prize."

These men were from different walks of life and no one looked the same. Jim was the tallest and was a school principal; Tom, an older gentleman with white hair, owned a local coffee shop; Joey was a chef and Jerry a schoolteacher. And of course, me!

After designing the costumes and assembling the props and everything else we needed, the big night finally arrived. When our turn came, we appeared on stage in an old Duesenberg convertible car replete with uniformed doorman and chauffeur. Our entrance music was from the classic Judy Garland and Fred Astaire film *Easter Parade*. The audience went wild. We loved every minute and won the Best Prize trophy. It was the first of many Puccio Productions to follow.

After years of being a contestant, I was invited to be a GGRC judge along with Orin. I couldn't help thinking at the time: I'd rather be on stage—in costume.

The early '70s weren't all good times, however—two tragedies struck my family during that period.

After I left home to begin my new life with Jim and following my mother's death, I never had anything to do with either brother, Joe or Phillip. We were so different from each other. Perhaps they resented me because I was gay. Surely, when I moved in with Jim, it became obvious. I was so different from my brothers in temperament and interests. I don't know what they really thought of me. I do know, and sad to say, there was no love lost between us.

Phillip had always been predisposed to getting into trouble. My mother would go to school and deal with his problematic behavior. He was caught on several occasions smoking in the boys' bathroom with other kids. He was suspended and could not graduate with the rest of the class.

In 1971 I was living in Beverly Hills when I received a phone call saying Phillip was tragically killed in a car accident. He was only twenty-three years old and had served two years in the Army, graduated from college, and was coaching football and teaching at the university in Birmingham. Sixteen people were injured that day and three lost their lives.

It was a devastating event for my family, especially for my sister Marietta. She had lost her mother when she was eleven and now her brother. Being close in age, they spent many formative years at home together and were so close, especially after I left home. Marietta suffered his death more than the rest of the family. The shock of his passing pushed her into a debilitating state of juvenile diabetes at the age of eighteen.

Phillip never got a chance to realize his ambitions and complete his life's journey. At the time, he had a lot going for him. He was a big, handsome, smart young man who simply had been targeted unfairly by fate. I never got to know him.

Another tragedy struck my family that same year with the loss of my brother-in-law Robert. A heavy smoker, he was diagnosed with pancreatic cancer after seventeen years of marriage and died within a few weeks. My sister Sarah was heartbroken. She could not believe the change that was taking place in her life, being widowed at an early age with two young daughters. Robert had been in the Navy, so fortunately Sarah, as his widow, was left with veterans' benefits. I always believed she adored her husband, the only man in her life.

Sarah asked me to leave Los Angeles and come back to Birmingham. I told her I couldn't do that.

My professional life changed in 1974. Dan Baker, the manager of the design firm Cannell & Chaffin, phoned me at Robinson's. My reputation was preceding me as a young, talented interior designer, and I was clearly under scrutiny and open to a new job opportunity.

"Bernardo, would you consider coming to work at Cannell's?" Dan asked. I was in his office the next day. Dan gave me an offer I couldn't refuse. It was double the amount I was receiving at Robinson's. Cannell & Chaffin was the most prestigious interior design firm in California. I was being asked to join its staff of forty accomplished designers.

Bidding farewell to Robinson's was not an easy decision. The company had been good to me—six years of hard work and indelibly significant experience acquired, not to mention many good friends gathered along the way. Mr. Glick, then president of Robinson's, attempted to change my mind. I was resolute. It was time for me to move on. We parted on good terms.

Before long, a friend and coworker of mine, Darlene, recommended a trip to Europe in September 1974. I told her the idea was wonderful but that such a trek was not in my current budget. I was feeling uncomfortable about spending frivolously. Drinking and partying at the Garden District was far more affordable.

As luck would have it, though, Darlene told me her boyfriend was richer than Roosevelt and that he would pay for everything; he simply didn't want her to travel alone. My trip to Europe would be completely subsidized. How could I refuse the temptation? I could not and did not.

"Sign me up," I said to Darlene.

As it turned out, Darlene's mystery boyfriend was married, and had a family. She was the mistress. He liked to keep her occupied and happy. So, our journey began with a flight to New York where we stayed at The Plaza Hotel, while Darlene's boyfriend and his wife stayed at The Pierre. I came to love our mysterious benefactor if only because of his incredible generosity.

Darlene was an attractive blonde but didn't know how to put

herself together. I took her shopping at Bloomingdale's and Saks Fifth Avenue to get her appropriately gussied up for the Big Apple. I selected some stylish daytime outfits and fashionable evening apparel. Most importantly, a cosmetician friend of mine at Saks showed Darlene how to properly apply her makeup. We dined at the famous 21 and the Stork Club. I obtained tickets to Broadway shows and we ended each night at a trendy club. Thanks to me, Darlene looked stunning and we both had a wonderful time. It pleased me immensely that I could contribute to her happiness since she was showing me such generosity and friendship.

After three exhaustive days in New York, we flew to Paris. There, a certain routine kicked in for both of us. She would spend afternoons with her boyfriend and I would hit the gay bars or bathhouses. We didn't speak any French, which was a bit of an annoyance, but it did not diminish the joy factor at all. We toured the Louvre and the Arc de Triomphe and strolled along the banks of the Seine, not to mention scaling the Eiffel Tower by way of the elevator. We remained in Paris for four days and then it was time for Rome!

Rome was fascinating not only for its physical beauty but because of its undeniable historical significance. Seeing ruins over two thousand years old was extraordinary. Being a bit of a history buff, I took in the wonders of this ancient city with enthusiasm and intellectual abandon. Here in Rome, as well, Darlene and I enjoyed our routine of regular sex—she with her boyfriend, me with whatever gay outlets were available. I was adept at getting into mischief, and reveled in it. This included a passionate one-night stand with a very handsome young man I met in a bar. His name was Michael and I invited him to join Darlene and me for dinner at our hotel, The Eden, at the top of the Spanish steps. He stayed the night and in the morning we said our goodbyes. Darlene and I were leaving for Florence.

After a full day of travel by bus, in the rain, and stopping at the Tuscan hill towns of Siena and Perugia, we finally arrived at our hotel, the Excelsior, exhausted but happy. The desk clerk approached me.

"Mr. Puccio," he said, "you have a gentleman waiting for you in the lobby."

I was surprised, for who could possibly know me here in Florence?

To my great surprise, the gentleman was my boy toy from Rome. He had driven his motorcycle, in the pouring rain, all the way from Rome to Florence just to see me. I must have told him not only where we were going, but also where we were staying.

Darlene looked at me and said, "You must have made an impression." It was a lovely reunion and we spent the night together.

As Darlene planned her trip to Montecatini Terme to enjoy the spas, my sights were on Amsterdam—a place I shall always remember fondly. Darlene and I said our farewells to one another, vowing to meet up upon our return to Los Angeles.

Amsterdam, plain and simple, was just too damned much fun. I met several attractive men, all blond, and had fabulous sex with one and all. I also enjoyed the museums and historical sites of interest. What I noted most of all being in Holland was how alone I was. There was no longer a Jim at my side, nor a buddy like Darlene to keep me company. I was rogue at this point. It struck me how ironic my life was up to now. Not yet thirty years old and I'd traveled to Europe, met my childhood idol Lana Turner, and was a rising Beverly Hills interior designer.

After four days with the Dutch, it was time to head home. I longed for the land of eternal sunshine. I was exhausted yet terribly happy and wonderfully fulfilled on every level imaginable. This trip had been exquisite in every way. I will always cherish my first trip to Europe.

⊰14⊱

Making it Dance

I THOUGHT THAT, UPON my return, the one creature that would act happy to see me would be my poodle, GG. In this, I was to be terribly disappointed. GG was pissed off something fierce because I left him for almost three weeks—and let me know it in due course. We adored each other and had never been apart for any length of time. I held him close and begged for his forgiveness. He was in truth very happy to see me—notwithstanding my temporary abandonment of him, poor baby.

I was back at Cannell & Chaffin the very next day, but dragging. I needed a vacation from my vacation. Well, that's how I felt—a happy kind of tired. I had literally screwed my way across most of the European continent, but now it was time to get back to work and actualize my life plan.

I must emphasize, besides the sexual escapades, the most fulfilling part of my trip across the Continent was my acquisition of education. All the museums I frequented, absorbing beautiful and ancient art and appreciating exquisite architecture, which had withstood the trauma of centuries—the great enjoyment with these kinds of memories is that they may be relived repeatedly, sometimes in different mental contexts. Not so easily done with sexual remembrance wherein the explosive moment of climax is too ephemeral to latch on to mentally for more than a few seconds. Not to diminish this enjoyment factor, it was simply different from reflections on great art, history, and classical Ionic and Doric architecture.

But I ramble on. Forgive me.

I decided upon my return that I would buy property.

At thirty years old, I figured, I deserved a house.

My grandfather, whom I adored, had left me some money upon his passing. It wasn't a huge sum, but it was a start, and in the early 1970s the real estate market had not gone crazy yet. There were still good buys to be had out there.

The house I chose was a $60,000, two-bedroom Mediterranean bungalow on North Harper Avenue in Hollywood that seemed ideal. The money my grandfather left me would cover the deposit. What I was not prepared for was the additional $5,000 I needed to cover the cost of escrow. Consequently, I bit the bullet and decided to call my father, whom I had not spoken with since my mother's death. I blamed him for her death. After many years, I realized that my mother lived her life the way she wanted. She loved her husband and her family, and it was her choice to work so hard.

"Dad, it's me," I said. "I called because I'm buying a house, my first house, and I need $5,000 to close the deal. Will you send it to me?"

This was the first time I had ever asked my father for anything. I had always gone to my mother. Dad was emotionally cold. Rarely was there verbal communication between us. He was a macho Italian man who rarely spoke.

"Of course, Bernard," he said simply. "What is your address?"

With a sigh of relief, I gave him my information and said, "Thank you."

I bought the house and could not have been happier.

It seemed now that I had everything.

Well, everything except love.

Jim had been more a case of youthful codependency commingled with natural adoration of one who cared for another so greatly. True love? No, that had not yet been part of my life to date. However, I was still looking.

Little did I know how soon another piece of good fortune would come my way.

⇥15⇤

Orin Kennedy

Garden District Crowd

B<small>Y THE TIME</small> my early thirties arrived, I was fairly well established.

My social life was stellar, my work was going gung-ho, and the Garden District lived and breathed sex, sex, sex.

Nonetheless, a noticeable vacuum in my life existed and it hit me at my emotional and spiritual core. I wanted more than transitory sexual gratification. I wanted someone special in my life.

One evening, I walked into the Garden District, as usual. My friend, Tom Walsh, was speaking to a tall, attractive blond fellow. Tom turned to me, already buzzed, and said: "Bernardo, I want you to meet Orin Kennedy." They had just met at the bar.

I smiled at Orin. My first impression was that he was physically my type. My second thought was that I was feeling that legendary "spark" I'd heard so much of, but never experienced.

"Orin Kennedy," I said aloud. "A pleasure."

Orin was exceedingly polite, a quality that only enhanced an already life-threatening New York charm. I agreed to indulge my curiosity and Orin's insistence on having a few drinks. I continued to be mesmerized by my new acquaintance and the night was delightful, but I eventually needed to excuse myself.

"Orin, forgive me, but my friend Bill Clutter is coming in from Washington, DC, tomorrow. However, if you'd like to join us for dinner here at the Garden District, tomorrow night, that would be great."

"Sounds wonderful," Orin replied without hesitation.

Orin and me

Orin was in real estate at the time we began dating and, to be fair, we did not experience a whirlwind romance. I continued to date other people, and I'm confident that Orin did the same. We enjoyed one another's company immensely and this galvanized something in both of us that lent itself to our continued relationship.

I was wildly involved in my new passion—flipping houses for a profit. My first house on Harper Avenue, for which I had paid $60,000, was enjoying market interest. I had invested very little money in its restoration and, before I knew it, I was offered $96,000 from a buyer who was extremely motivated. Thanks to the wise counsel of Papa Ben, I well understood that pay and play in the real estate world could well be profitable, and I accepted the offer without hesitation. The profit made me deliriously happy, but now I was faced with the pressing question of what to do next.

Orin and I had lunch one day at the Garden District.

"Bernardo, I have a house on the market up in the Hollywood Hills. It's a fixer-upper with a fabulous view. Would you be interested in seeing it?"

In truth, I had less than zero interest in such a viewing but agreed to look at it anyway due to my increasing fondness for Orin. I was enjoying his company immensely—his kindness, his overall manner, and his piercing intelligence continued to be an irresistible turn-on for me and saying no to him was difficult on every level.

To my great surprise, the house on Laurel View Drive was a rather spectacular piece of property, boasting a panoramic view of Hollywood and Century City. It was a small house and needed work, but this did not diminish my enthusiasm or my ultimate decision to make an immediate offer to purchase the place for $90,000. My offer was accepted and Orin and I celebrated our win-win situation with gusto.

Orin and I continued to date, but I was still not ready to settle down in earnest. The voice in my head insisted that I was not pre-pared for such a commitment.

The Laurel View house was a true fixer-upper. It needed every-thing, inside and out. The plus factor of this property was that it had an incredible southern panoramic view. I used lots of mirrors to make the rooms seem larger and also to reflect the view. I chose a monochromatic color scheme, beige and ivory with my signature accent of black, and had the exterior of the house painted beige with dark beige trim. It looked like a model home.

The house was situated on top of a hill with thirty steps going up from the street to the front door. I was very young, so the steps didn't bother me. This was the only entrance. I had the terraced gardens replanted with a ground cover, which grew in quickly, and looked beautiful all year round. The garage was located on the street level. Directly above the garage was a sun deck—great for entertaining.

I threw grand parties while enjoying my success in all areas of my life. Furthermore, I'd met a young man around this time by the name of Ken. To be sure, I still felt committed to Orin and our dating arrangement, but Ken fairly knocked me off my feet from, if nothing else, a purely sexual level. It was, quite simply, the best sex I'd ever had and, of course, I was infatuated. He moved in quickly, against my better judgment.

Ken—I can't even remember his last name—worked as a phone operator for an answering service. In the 1970s, this was a fairly common form of employment, if not terribly glamorous. Ken and I enjoyed ourselves immensely. I liked showing him off. This time I had a trophy boy, versus being one. In reality, his inordinate drug use was a major problem I could not tolerate. Ours was not going to be a lasting relationship, but it was fun for a while. After a year we decided it was best to separate. I hope he's still alive—he was a beautiful person.

This was a period in my life when my personal health began to deteriorate. I'd been diagnosed with hepatitis B and was severely ill for the better part of three months. The drinking ceased and I devoted myself to the care of a good physician and homeopathic remedies. This went on for months wherein I was so ill I was forced into a six-month leave of absence from work. My discipline to health and recovery paid off as my body was able to kill the virus. However, it was a temporary fix. The long-term effect on my liver was devastating.

My life, unfortunately, revolved around drinking. It was, besides my work and sexual excesses, my most notable public identity. Thus, after six months of alcoholic abstinence, I started drinking again—not the smartest choice. However, I was feeling and looking better, in full social swing, and was back at work concentrating on my career.

All was good for a while.

I was back to my crazy lifestyle in no time.

Orin was still a significant figure in my life.

Meanwhile, during this serious period of my life and its associated drama, through many boyfriends, lovers, and getting sick with hepatitis, I always had my beautiful poodle GG with me. He was my best friend and companion for over fifteen years. Unfortunately, his health was also beginning to fail, due to age.

One night I came home with his dinner. He only ate food from restaurants, never store-bought dog food. Very spoiled. I fed him as usual, but this time he began choking. I tried to alleviate the problem, but after a couple of minutes his body became lifeless. I don't know what happened. A friend and I rushed him to the vet, but it was too late. GG was gone. What a horrible time and a tragic loss for me. GG will never be forgotten.

Loosing GG was a devastating event. I was also closing the door on my connection to Jim. After all he had given GG to me. Everyone knew how upset I was. They sent cards and flowers like he was a person. I felt so lonely. I truly grieved his death and miss him still.

⊰16⊱
The Puccio Signature

AT LENGTH, I decided to sell my house on Laurel View at a good profit. I moved from home ownership to contented renter. I found an apartment in West Hollywood, known as "Boys Town" at the time. Soon after, I met a man named John Whyte. He had bought a house in the Hollywood Hills and I had given his place a stylish redo. John was a super queen from New York and I liked him from day one. He'd been a top male model back in the 1960s and made a ton of money. Further impressing me, John owned the Fire Island Pines Botel off the south shore of Long Island, New York, long a vacation destination catering to the gay celebrity crowd.

John and I became fast friends. He invited me to visit Fire Island for a brief respite from the real world. Never one to easily resist a chance to travel to someplace I've never been, I accepted without hesitation. I'd always heard about the wild sexual escapades on Fire Island. The abundance of free sex, without commitment . . . I had no choice.

"John," I said rather coyly. "I look forward to my new adventure on the island."

"You won't regret it, Bernardo," John said with a wink, and I believed him.

That summer, I flew to New York to indulge in a combined business and pleasure trip. Then from the Big Apple, I ferried over to Fire Island.

Well, it was like Charlie being dropped into the middle of Willie Wonka's Chocolate Factory. It was better than anything I could have imagined. I spent five days on this fantasy island and loved every moment of it. I had returned to my old ways. Sex fell literally in my lap. I was denied nothing. The men…the men were sublimely gorgeous. I was in paradise.

I met one young man during my visit who had absolutely no objections to nonstop sex, without complication, without commitment.

We spent a wonderful two days together; I was surprised after we parted to later learn he was a priest, serving at a parish in New York City.

When it was time for me to leave, John informed me that he'd had many houseguests in the past, but never one as active as myself. I took this exalted compliment to heart.

"Thank you, John," I said coyly. "Nicest thing anyone has ever said to me!"

Returning to Los Angeles and still working at Cannell & Chaffin, I tabulated the number of rather stellar, high-profile clients I had brought in from my former place of work, Robinson's. The owner of the company told me I was the best designer in the house.

That little voice, which occasionally whispered to me in my mind, was saying, "Perhaps it's time to move on, Bernardo." However, I felt any immediate decisions should be put on hold.

All my life I've enjoyed the company of women. I appreciated their intelligence, beauty, and sensitivity. I've had longtime relationships with so many women. They knew I was gay but that didn't matter.

In the late '70s, a mutual friend introduced me to a very attractive blonde. I will not mention her name. She was going through a divorce. I would see her at parties and eventually we exchanged phone numbers. I enjoyed her friendship. We would speak regularly on the phone and sometimes have lunch.

One night, I picked her up at her Beverly Hills home and we went out to dinner at a charming little French restaurant in West Hollywood. It's still there—Café D'Etoile, now a gay café and bar.

While dining and conversing for some time, she began to slur her words. She also got very cozy and relaxed at the table. A strange, almost uncomfortable feeling came over me. Suddenly I felt her hand on my lap. I tried redirecting what was happening to no avail. Finally, I just looked at her and said, "You do know I'm gay?"

She looked at me and said, in a soft whispery voice, "It doesn't matter. I find you attractive and sexy."

After moving her hand away, I let her know it was time to leave. I asked the waiter for the check and we departed. As I was driving her home, she began telling me how unhappy she was in her marriage and that she was glad to be getting a divorce. I felt sorry for this beautiful lady who was so unhappy. When I pulled up to her home, she asked me to help her to the door. She was feeling the wine. I wasn't feeling any pain either; I had had several cocktails myself.

I thought it proper to escort her to the door. She asked me to come in for a minute. When she turned on the lights and came over to me, I thought she was going to thank me, but she started kissing me. Memories of Lana Turner!

I politely said, "I'm not interested," turned around, and walked out the front door, truly feeling sorry for her. I certainly did not want a repeat performance of the Lana Turner experience. Once was enough!

Soon after, I met a very amiable client, Leon Lindenbaum, and his charming wife, Patricia. He had commissioned me to decorate their condo in Beverly Hills, and we developed not only a highly satisfying professional relationship, but a personal one as well. We had become good friends. Leon was a smart businessman who bought condos in Palm Springs and the contiguous cities of Rancho Mirage and Palm Desert throughout the 1970s. We had a good thing going back then; he'd provide the capital to buy the condos and I in turn would renovate and decorate them in a desert-appropriate style. We made an effective team. At the time we were working on an agreeable percentage basis, but the day finally came when he made me an irresistible offer.

"Bernardo, think seriously about joining me in an equal partnership. I'll continue to buy property and you decorate. We'll split the profit fifty-fifty!"

"Leon, of course I'm interested," I stammered. This is all too good to be true, I thought to myself. "Let me speak to my lawyer and I'll get back to you."

"Okay, but don't take too much time. The housing market is hot. We can make some serious money!"

"Sounds good, Leon."

The partnership was, of course, invoked and solidified to everyone's satisfaction. Leon and I continued to flip properties, all of which made substantial profits.

I remember enjoying a private moment in my apartment one evening, congratulating myself. "Bernardo," I said aloud, "you've come a long way from Birmingham. You've done well. Very good, Bernardo."

My life had exceeded every expectation I had ever dreamed of. On any given day of the week, I could be seen driving my beautiful white Cadillac convertible on my way east to Palm Springs. Life was more than good—it was amazing on every level. Sex was commonplace and plentiful. Mind you, I was still seeing Orin, but my sense of freedom would not be contained. I knew it couldn't last forever, but for the present I couldn't give a damn and continued to party.

The day finally came when I gave Cannell & Chaffin notice I would be leaving to strike out on my own. My reputation in Palm Springs was growing. Leon and I were making a killing in the condo market, and I firmly believed that a nine-to-five job for me was now a thing of the  past. However, life was about to throw me a helluva curveball.

The change arrived via the gas shortage crisis of the 1970s. The crisis directly affected the housing market in Palm Springs, which began to crumble fast. It had not fully hit Los Angeles yet, but the writing was on the wall. More change was coming and I would need to make some serious decisions.

The grind of the Palm Springs commute was beginning to wear on me. Economic downturn was in the air, so I kept on working, always looking for new opportunities. A realtor friend of mine called me one day.

"Listen, there's a great house coming on the market. It's just north of Sunset Boulevard on Queens Road. I think you might be interested. Would you like to have a look?"

I shrugged and replied, "Sure. Why not?"

After all, if I hated the house, I could simply say no.

The house was Mediterranean in style with beautiful gardens, a pool, and three bedrooms. It needed renovation, but I could see the promise of the place. After some serious thought, I put in an offer, which was quickly accepted.

I was now the proud owner of a fine house on Queens Road in the Hollywood Hills. My life at the moment could not have been more perfect!

It was a beautiful summer's day. I was at the Santa Palm Car Wash in West Hollywood waiting for my car to be finished when a black Rolls Royce convertible pulls up beside me. At the wheel was a good-looking Latin actor who I recognized immediately. He said, "How are you?" We made small conversation, and then he asked if I would like to go for a drink. I was used to this kind of periodic attention, so it was not a surprise. I said, "Sure, soon as I get my car."

"Where would you like to go?" he asked.

Wasting no time, I said, "I live just up from Sunset on Queens Road." He nodded in the affirmative.

I gave him my address and said, "I'll meet you up there."

And we did!

We saw each other many times after that day. He was a great-looking, successful actor, but I also knew he was married. That never bothered me before, but I felt this relationship was getting too serious. Since he was recognizable, we were discreet about being seen together.

One day we met in a small café where I regularly liked to have lunch, very charming and quiet. I noticed, after a couple of drinks, he became quite talkative and started asking lots of questions. I wasn't used to him being so interested in my life, other than sex. After conversing for a couple of hours, he mentioned something about his wife and her career. I asked, "What did she do?" He proceeded to tell me, and it turned out, I personally knew her. This came as a big shock!

I was used to dating married men. It didn't bother me. However, I never knew their wives. This was a turning point in our relationship. As much as I did not want to end the affair, I realized I must. Also, I was beginning to really enjoy being with him. He was very bright and a perfect gentleman, but the last thing I wanted to do was break up his marriage and destroy their lives. He was beginning to fall in love with me. I decided to break it off; I could not see him anymore. He was shocked. That was the end of our romance.

Every time I would see his wife, I felt guilty and still do. I was sad when I read he had passed. He was a wonderful guy, and I enjoyed our time together.

❧ 17 ☙

Aids—The Gay Cancer

By 1981 ORIN and I were an official item. We were two of a kind in spirit, with totally different dispositions. He was the nice Jewish boy and I was the tough Sicilian. Well, an exaggeration perhaps—but if I didn't like you, I simply deprived you of my company.

People around us were getting sick and dying. Although we never verbally pledged to be faithful, it became an unspoken result of the AIDS epidemic that was about to consume a large portion of gay society, including close friends and family.

The US economy experienced a serious recession. These were tough times. I was forced to lease out the Queens Road house, which had become a financial burden. My design business slowed down to the point where, in order to make a living, I took a position at Glabman's Furniture in Costa Mesa with lousy hours and a long commute.

Over time the effects of tax cuts and increased defense spending promoted a slow recovery. I was able to leave Glabman's after two months and concentrate on my own design business. My best friend, Nannell, now married to a successful international garment manufacturer, bought a townhouse condo in Westwood and asked me to

completely design and decorate the place from scratch. This was the major turning point in my career—it put my "Black-Tie" design style on the map.

The lessees on Queens Road took up their option to buy my house and life continued to move positively forward. By this time Orin had left real estate and was forging a new career in television as a location manager. With a strengthening economy, the future looked bright.

However, the world was undergoing a significant and historical metamorphosis. There was now talk of something obliquely sinister, known simply as "The Gay Cancer," which was killing friends and associates. The disease was proclaimed by professionals at the Centers for Disease Control and Prevention (CDC) to be transmitted primarily through sexual contact. I took note and decided on some immediate lifestyle alterations. After all, I'd had copious amounts of sex around the world. It was time for a change.

That change, of course, was not something that needed an overnight dynamic. Obviously it was Orin, my constant and ever-reliable companion for five years. We decided to solidify our relationship by my moving into his apartment on Harper Avenue.

The first year was admittedly difficult—that kind of transition required a period of adjustment. We were past the "honeymoon" stage; we were two individuals with different personalities and backgrounds. I was used to having my own space, controlling finances, and having the freedom to come and go as I pleased. Combining households and compromise were big changes for me.

However, we survived it. I was finally living sensibly, though this alteration to my former lifestyle was definitely not easy. Whereas, in the past, I could come and go freely with as many sexual partners as I wanted—living the perpetual Fire Island lifestyle—now I was responsible for and to one person, someone I loved dearly. My perfect companion whom I had always been searching for was there all the time.

We decided at length to buy a home together—our home, jointly. We were still living in his West Hollywood apartment when a realtor I knew told me of a new condo building on Westbourne Drive, also in West Hollywood, that we must see. I wanted a corner three-bedroom, but it had been sold, so we settled on a two-bedroom with a fabulous view of downtown Los Angeles. We bought it and I began decorating our home. Our home! Until now, the thought of "ours" was incomprehensible for freedom-loving Puccio.

We both agreed the style of our home should be contemporary. Orin met my predilection for plenty of mirrors and silk wall coverings without objection. Carpeting, of course, would be monochromatic with tasteful accessories and punctuations of color in artwork to complete the look.

I used our home as the model of what Puccio Designs was all about. It was a great selling point with potential clients. My work at this time was being highlighted in such magazines as *Designers West*, *Architectural Digest*, and *LA Magazine*, not to mention a few international publications well renowned in the field of interior design.

> *"Celebrates the restoration of black to its 20's splendor and prominence. Bernardo Puccio has created yet another interior design tribute to the 'grand' lifestyle."*
> —*Florida Design*

"A rich, luxurious quality achieved through the artistic use of mirrors, marble, and a subtle use of black and ivory are hallmarks of a Bernardo Puccio 'black-tie' interior. One of the most sought after design professionals in America."
—*Dimensions*

"Sparking sophistication."
—*Designers West*

Orin and I were on every invitation list to all the Beverly Hills celebrity and charity events. We were known as the "gay couple" and did nothing to hide this title. I was the superstar interior designer known for the Black-Tie approach. Tasteful and Elegant. My client list consisted of the rich and famous: Danny and Rosemarie Thomas, Telly Savalas, Steve and Leslie Crane, and many corporate CEOs.

Life was wonderful.
Business was great.
I was in full force with stellar and elevated career success.

Meanwhile, the "gay cancer" spread. It was a mysterious disease that, bluntly stated, seemed like it was targeted at homosexuals. Most of our

friends knew nothing of this contagion from a scientific standpoint, but we did know it was a killer. Our friends were dying. The symptoms of the disease were no less onerous: skin lesions, loss of weight, pulmonary disorders—the list went on and on about the early and late stages of this god damned disease.

When you think of a phrase like "gay cancer" and what it immediately invokes, the emotional and psychological effect on a person is monumental. It's bad enough to hear the dreaded proclamation "You have cancer." Can you imagine how it feels to hear a more oriented-specific terminology of "targeted"—targeted at you specifically as a gay individual? Imagine, if you will, hearing a phrase like "a blonde-haired, blue-eyed targeted cancer" or "an Asian male cancer that was, in every case, terminal and incurable." Suddenly, people would not come near you. You would become an instant social pariah—discriminated against solely because you've been targeted.

All we knew at this moment was that this illness, this plague, was targeting the gay community, and not just single-borne but in a mass-murder type of disease complicity.

In 1983, the Centers for Disease Control and Prevention (CDC) attached a name to the gay cancer—AIDS: acquired immune deficiency syndrome. It ostensibly attacked the immune system and exposed the body to a host of bacterial and viral evils that in fairly short order killed you hard-and-fast. It was still widely regarded as a gay cancer—erroneously so, as intravenous drug users, victims of contaminated blood transfusions, newly born infants, and others were also not spared; though, in greater proportion, AIDS hit gay males. This statistic could not be disputed. AIDS was transmitted, in large part, through the exchange of fluids and thereby primarily sexually. The discordance within the gay community proliferated on an exponential level, and the perception by the greater population was that we, as gay men, were evil devils who were simply getting what we deserved for our perversion and degenerate behavior. This was the greater part of a belief system engendered by a narrowly fixated Judeo-Christian far right.

Such madness in thinking and perception was wider than you might believe.

Worse, the government was taking little notice and this was in part due to the ineffective response by the president, Ronald Reagan. This level of indifference prevailed on both the local and federal level of governance. Only the CDC had the correct response to how AIDS was transmitted, and it wasn't by exposure in a swimming pool or shaking hands. For most of America, if you contracted AIDS, you were a leper, to be shunned like a biblical pestilence.

The media was no less helpful. They either deliberately or through sheer ignorance conflated this disease to be one solely confined to the homosexual community. The backlash to us as gay men was damning and agonizing.

We decided to fight back and accepted the call to battle. The responsibility now rested on the shoulders of an already ostracized group—the American men and women who were gay and now dying in droves. Many Americans at the time would probably have preferred we go back in the closet and turn the clock back to 1950, where all this dirtiness need not be confronted on a daily basis. As those of us in the gay community well knew, there was no going back. Homophobia was out of control. AIDS patients were being quarantined in hospitals all over the country, largely left to die, wasting away alone. No medical treatments or funding at the time were being adequately researched.

Activist groups sprung up nationwide, demanding medical assistance. Gradually, the media started to pay attention to the epidemic that was consuming so many—primarily those in the arts. When film icon Rock Hudson announced in 1985 that he had, and was dying from, AIDS, the shock and dismay rattled through the chambers of both Hollywood and Washington. Elizabeth Taylor entered the theater of this war shortly after Rock's pronouncement.

It was Elizabeth who threw her hat into the ring at a time when it mattered most. That hat was literally worth millions in revenue and research. Here, we had an advocate in the media—a film legend—who was both beloved and respected and who showed up not just to write checks but to put her face out there, a poster child of fame and fortune as a warrior against both an unjust disease and a prejudicial public that needed education rather than coddling. This was a game changer.

Elizabeth once stated, and I paraphrase here:

> When I saw the kind of hypocrisy that was going on, I thought it was terrible. So many in the gay community had helped me in my own career and the careers of others—yet, now, in a time of crisis, Hollywood was largely turning its back on its gay brothers and sisters. I was well known and wanted to retire but the tabloids wouldn't let me. So I said, fine, if you're going to screw me over, I'll use you as well."

Powerful stuff.

In the summer of 1985, my secretary told me I had a call from APLA (AIDS Project Los Angeles). The representative asked if I would be interested in being a part of a commitment dinner to raise money for AIDS research—as the de facto designer of the event.

I knew that Elizabeth Taylor was the chairperson of the event and I gave a resounding yes to the offer. I adored Elizabeth. She galvanized the Hollywood community, of course, but she was shrewd and savvy enough to realize that she needed to garner favor and support from the scientific community as well.

Due to her organization and diligence, Elizabeth was able to gain the support of Dr. Mathilde Krim who, with a small group of associates, co-founded amfAR (American Foundation for AIDS Research) with Elizabeth as Founding International Chairperson. She was a genuine leader and eventually elicited the aid of other early heroes, such as thirteen-year-old Ryan White, who had contracted AIDS following a blood transfusion, playwright and AIDS activist Larry Kramer, and Elizabeth Glaser, wife of actor Paul Michael Glaser, who suffered from AIDS herself due to a tragic case of a contaminated blood transfusion.

I remember so well the first day I got to meet Elizabeth Taylor. I had received an invitation to attend a special meeting at the popular restaurant Trumps in West Hollywood to discuss the first AIDS fundraiser "Commitment to Life." I truly did not know what to expect. This was my initial involvement with an organizational fundraiser.

After an hour of cocktails and getting to know each other, Elizabeth arrived. She exited her limo accompanied by two gentlemen and her private secretary. Elizabeth was very suntanned. She had just gotten back from Puerto Vallarta, Mexico, dressed in a navy-and-white outfit and pearls. My meeting with her was an experience the likes of which I had never felt before. It was a royal feeling that you never forget. Looking into her violet eyes was like entering another dimension. Unforgettable! She spoke in a kind, gentle, and humble voice.

After conversing with me for a few minutes, with so many other committee members present, Elizabeth personally thanked me in advance for my interior design participation. I would have the pleasure of designing the interiors for this gala fundraiser and working with this legendary star to raise awareness and money for AIDS.

How did she get celebrities to attend this important event, that I was enjoined to beautify on every level? Truth be told, many of her celeb pals simply told her "No!" Elizabeth was initially shocked by the bigotry, but this passed in a flash and she got to the business at hand. She got on the phone and began to enlist the Hollywood elite. Said Taylor at the time: "I have never had so many 'no's' said to me. They didn't want to come to the event, didn't want to associate themselves with it. Some folks not only slammed doors in my face, but I received actual death threats. Something had happened to the world and it emanated from pure, raw terror."

On a personal level, to be part of a world-changing endeavor and working with Elizabeth Taylor to save so many lives using my talent meant more than anything I could have done for monetary or celebrity gain. I felt like an integral component, a champion for good.

I was privileged to meet Elizabeth—another movie star I had idolized with the hope of one day meeting, forget about working side by side on such a humanitarian cause. She was a driven woman committed to a cause outside herself, the antithesis of Lana Turner. Her vision for a better world precluded her material needs on every level. In truth, she restored my faith in humanity and continues to do so every time I reflect on her dedication. I will always hold a special place for her in my heart. My time with Elizabeth was like a dream come true. She had always been my idol—and always will be.

From my perspective, working for the cause offered personal reward hard to describe. True, it meant recognition but here was a chance to use and apply my sense of perfectionism to something far greater than myself. I immediately collaborated with the APLA Committee on my vision of that special evening to come. My objective was to create the most fabulous night ever in Hollywood. To accommodate the anticipated 2,500 guest participants, venue options were limited. The Bonaventure hotel in downtown Los Angeles would be the choice. Invitations were deployed, a theme implemented, and I went to work. Sleep no longer was a factor in my life except as an impediment.

I took a calculated risk. I chose an Egyptian theme in the entry and corridor in honor of Cleopatra, once portrayed by Elizabeth Taylor in the film by the same name. The visual was striking. One after the other, the guests arrived to honor former first lady Betty Ford, who founded the Betty Ford Center, the acclaimed drug and alcohol rehabilitation clinic, which Elizabeth went to in 1983. Many were there, if not to precisely support the cause, to support Taylor: Marlo Thomas, Phil Donahue, Cher, Burt Reynolds, Shirley MacLaine, Burt Lancaster, Carol Burnett, Sammy Davis, Jr., Rod Stewart, Whoopi Goldberg, Cyndi Lauper. Their presence meant funding.

The evening was a spectacular success! As a thank you to the event committee, Elizabeth hosted a small dinner party a week or two later.

She thanked me for my participation and dedication. We would do it all again the following year at the Page Museum at the La Brea Tar Pits—and more to follow.

In 1991 Elizabeth Taylor established the Elizabeth Taylor AIDS Foundation, which supports direct care services for people living with AIDS worldwide as well as funding HIV education. I feel honored that I was able to have been part of that movement for change. I share Elizabeth's opinion that even if only one more person suffers from AIDS, the fight continues.

I still don't know how Elizabeth Taylor got to me. I always felt very privileged to know her and to have worked on several AIDS benefits. I treasure her personal "thank you" letters. They are framed and hanging on my office wall along with my life's greatest memories. There will never be another Elizabeth Taylor. Her unforgettable caring and giving of herself to the AIDS cause will always be honored. To that effort, and to this day, I remain committed to the cause.

ᵈᶦAIDS Benefit 1985ᵈᵉ

Diahann Carroll and Stevie Wonder

Michael J. Fox and Orin Kennedy

Whoopi Goldberg

Marlo Thomas and Phil Donahue

Ricardo Montalban and Roddy McDowall

Steve Kmetko and Grace Robbins

Rip Taylor

❧18❧
Cristal Puccio

BEFORE WE MET, Orin had a lover who could best be described as an intelligent and charming opportunist who led a rather daring life. His first name was Dan when I knew him, though he'd changed his name several times. He and Orin had met on Fire Island and were partners for a number of years. His capacity for making money was rather dubious. At this time, he was selling real estate and living in an apartment building next door to us. He and I became good friends, but I never trusted the guy. This did not diminish our friendship, but just as one might own a pet snake and never really go so far as to pet the damn thing for fear of getting bit, this was my relationship with Dan.

One Saturday afternoon, we all went to lunch. Out of the blue, Orin gets it into his head to check out a pet store at the Westside Pavilion in West Los Angeles. The mall housed the Animal Kingdom and I could tell that having lost two cats already, Orin was interested in acquiring another kitty. I indulged his longing that day and was surprised how that shopping indulgence would end.

We entered the pet shop, filled with dogs and cats. Suddenly, Orin's eyes fell upon a little white kitten. He waved me over and I checked out the little kitty. I melted like the Wicked Witch of the West. I wanted him immediately and voiced my desire to Orin. Orin's expression was downright comical. I could see anxiety and worry in his eyes. Orin knew that I was a proven impulse buyer, so he took me aside and recommended further discussion.

He warned me of the negatives of possessing a cat. They were independently clean creatures, preening constantly, but they had a tendency to make mistakes in the house and he knew how fastidious I was about cleanliness and my furnishings.

"You have no experience with cats," Orin said. "Let's go for a drink and talk about this some more. We need to discuss troublesome cat issues before we make a final decision."

So we hit a bar and talked over the kitty matter. I would not be deterred. I said I would take complete responsibility!

Orin surrendered. "Fine, but he's your responsibility." Orin later told me he wanted me to make the final decision to purchase the kitty so I could never throw the responsibility that comes with pet ownership on him alone.

I agreed. "I'll take care of him."

We returned to the shop and I saw my future kitty was being held by a large woman of indeterminate age. I waved to the friendly-looking salesperson who had assisted us earlier.

"Young man," I said, slipping a twenty-dollar bill into his hand. "Listen to me carefully. Go over and take that kitten out of that woman's hands, tell her he's already been sold, and bring the kitten to me. Then go fill out the necessary paperwork for the purchase."

The salesman executed these instructions perfectly, although I noticed some considerable agitation from the woman, who protested that the cat was meant for her—exactly what I thought she would do.

That is how we bought Cristal—to the tune of $1,000, including required accessories.

We never guessed at the time this precious little fur ball would be our prized possession for the next eighteen years.

Cristal adored Orin, of course—both were Gemini, creatures of multiple personalities. I dealt with them all. Cristal loved me, as I was the one who held him when those scary visits to our vet, Dr. Kidwell, were required.

Problems cropped up during our vacation months in May and December. Finding someone to care for our baby was challenging. Orin found a lovely and personable young woman whom we both liked and trusted. She assisted us in babysitting duties with Cristal for many years until she went off and got married. Thereafter, cat-sitting duties fell to Orin's location assistant, George.

I never wished to kennel Cristal. When Orin and I left town for a day or two, we left plenty of water and food. Cristal ate and drank sparingly. However, we were rewarded on our return with damp spots on a particular loveseat—a show of protest, no doubt, for us leaving him.

A dramatic event took place when I took Cristal to be shampooed. He was an inordinately unfussy cat and did not take to preening himself like most felines. So I dropped him off one day at the Animal Farm to be groomed, and was told to return in a few hours for pickup.

Orin and I killed the next few hours having lunch on Santa Monica Boulevard in West Hollywood before returning to pick up Cristal. I asked Orin to go in while I was double-parked. He complied and returned a few minutes later.

Orin put the carrying case in the back of my car. I turned to look at my Cristal.

Then I started screaming, "That's not Cristal. That's not my cat!"

I tore out of the car, leaving Orin slightly bewildered, and ran screaming into the shop. "Where the hell is my cat? You fuckers gave me the wrong cat!"

I must have terrified everyone, as my temper and vocal rage were obvious. The attendants finally realized they had given Cristal to another client. Then I remembered, as I was waiting in my car for Orin, I saw someone leave the shop who I recognized—a falling-down drunk on any given afternoon or evening. The store's owner assured me the matter would be resolved. He gave me his word. I quieted down somewhat and Orin and I tried to unwind at a bar nearby.

Several hours later the correct cats were remanded to their proper owners, but I doubt that any of the attendants at the grooming shop would soon forget the fury of Bernardo Puccio! In any event the erroneous cat exchange ended happily. They never saw us again.

❧19❧

West to Wilshire Boulevard

Orin AND I had each other, which was most important going
through such traumatic times. And now we were living life as if
it might suddenly end. In my case the prognosis was known and
dangerous.

The year was 1987. We had been living in our West Hollywood
condo for six years. I had just picked up my first Jaguar that I wanted
so badly, but I had not yet learned all of its mechanical features. It
was customized with a built-in phone. This was my dream car. I just
adored it.

Then suddenly one day I received a call from Orin while I was
driving. He sounded strange.

"Come quick. I think I'm having a heart attack!"

I said I would be there in five minutes. I was rushing, but for some reason the car lacked power. Suddenly I realized the emergency brake was on.

By the time I arrived home, the paramedics had already arrived and were checking Orin's vital signs. He was lying on the sofa in the study. He did not want to go to the hospital to be checked out, but one of the paramedics said he must go to make sure he wasn't having a heart attack. I remember Orin telling the man he had to attend a wrap party that he had organized and it was that night. He was working on the TV series *L.A. Law* at the time.

One of the paramedics responded, "If you don't go to the hospital, they may be going to your wrap party."

I immediately said, "Let's go!" Off we went to Cedars-Sinai. Orin's complexion was ashen. We were both scared. This was the first medical emergency of our lives together. What a traumatic experience for us both!

With medication, the elephant-on-the-chest pressure he was experiencing eventually subsided, but he refused to have an invasive angiogram. Three days later, while he was still in the hospital for observation, the chest pain returned with a vengeance. Before the medics rolled Orin into the operating room, I told him I loved him, which was a rare show of verbal affection on my part.

All went well with a double angioplasty, but complications arose. A nurse had given Orin too much heparin and he started to bleed internally. What should have been an overnight procedure ended up a two-week hospital stay. Orin was black and blue and in pain, from his chest to his knees including everything in between. It would take weeks for the discoloration and pain to disappear. Life would continue.

I had now become the condo king when it came to high-rise design. My client list had grown immensely. We were also making friends with the rich and famous and living the good life traveling the world. Winters in Acapulco, then cruising the Baltic and Mediterranean from Spain to Italy to Greece and on to Israel, Turkey, and Egypt, where we toured the great pyramid of Giza. Business trips included Paris and Hong Kong to purchase antiques. We also took vacations to Hawaii, and cruises to Alaska, the Panama Canal, and New England every chance we got. It was a reward for all our hard work.

We had a regular dining itinerary of LA restaurants: Friday lunch at the Bistro Gardens, Saturday night dinner at either Le Dome or Jimmy's, and Sundays at Matteo's, mingling with friends and celebrities, all the while both of us enjoying marvelous career success.

Several times a year Orin and I were invited to the Trousdale Estates home of philanthropists Hal and Cynthia Gershman to celebrate certain holidays. They were very charitable and social and gave wonderful parties, with lots of Hollywood names, especially comedians such as Danny Thomas, Milton Berle, Phyllis Diller, and Sid Caesar. There was always a surprise entertainer who would perform, like Natalie Cole and Wayne Newton.

It was at the Gershmans' annual July 4th dinner that I had the plea-sure of sitting next to the incredible Debbie Reynolds. We had a great time conversing. She loved her wine; I preferred vodka. Many of our crowd, at the time, were drinkers. As we were talking and enjoying the party, I told Debbie I had decorated her ex-husband Harry Karl's apartment. She laughed loudly and asked, "Did you get paid?" She was very surprised when I said yes. Harry had a penchant for fancy shoes and jewelry and had gambled away all of their money. He made a lot of money in the shoe business, but was an inveterate gambler, losing millions.

Suddenly, I choked on a piece of BBQ. Debbie saw what was hap-pening and asked if she could help. I was very embarrassed and got up and left the table. I ran into the kitchen. One of the staff saw me choking and started slapping me on the back. The piece of meat eventually popped out of my mouth. Oh my God, what a relief. I thought I was dying. After composing myself, I returned to the table and explained to Debbie what had happened. She was so attentive and we continued talking and drinking the night away. I also told her I attended my first Thalians Charity Ball back in 1970. Debbie and a group of young stars founded this charity to benefit children with mental health problems. Also, that's where I first met her best friend and then Thalians president, Ruta Lee.

My career was on fire. Through my friend Dino, a hairstylist, I was referred to one of his celebrity clients—Rosemarie Thomas, the wife of multitalented TV comedian Danny Thomas.

Working with Rosemarie and Danny Thomas was a lot of fun. They had a large Mediterranean villa in Beverly Hills. Villa Rosa, named after her, was a grand home with a Middle Eastern touch, in that Danny's heritage was Lebanese. She was a philanthropist, head-ing up the fund-raising organization for St. Jude's Research Hospital. Born Rose Marie Cassaniti in Detroit, Michigan, she met and mar-ried up-and-coming comic Danny Thomas while working as a radio singer. They had a wonderful life.

Debbie Reynolds

Ruta Lee

Rosie's family came from Sicily, like mine and we had lots in common. Quite the character, she could drink and curse like a sailor, and loved a good time, entertaining family and friends in her beautiful home. I enjoyed decorating for her. She desired everything that was unusual and expensive—my kind of client. We became good friends and the Thomases attended several of my parties.

In the '80s my life was a complete merry-go-round of social and charity events, and I loved every minute of it. I wouldn't change a thing or a moment of the booming '80s.

As I matured, my appearance changed. I now was told that I resembled a middle-aged Tony Curtis. This was a great compliment, as I always thought Tony was a very handsome actor.

One night Orin and I decided to have dinner at Spago, the original restaurant up on Sunset Boulevard. This was the place to be on Saturday night. Bernard, the maître d', was at the door and of course we were seated at my regular table. The place was packed.

These were the drinking days. After a few cocktails, and I do mean a few, I got up to go to the men's room. As I made my way through the crowded dining room of celebrities, I soon found myself face-to-face with Tony Curtis. I could not believe it. I felt I was looking at my reflection in the mirror, but years older. As our eyes met, we both smiled. We exchanged hellos. I said that everywhere I went people thought I was Tony Curtis.

I shook his hand and exclaimed, "Brothers!"

He looked at me and said, "Darling, you're a lot prettier."

At that he gave me a big hug and a high five and, laughing loudly, added, "Sisters!"

That was an unforgettable evening. Tony died a few years later. I was so glad to have had this chance meeting with such an amiable superstar.

Throughout the '80s I had the pleasure of working with many wonderful and interesting clients. Orin and I had met Harry and Marilyn Lewis at an annual Gershman July 4th party. They were the creators and owners of the Hamburger Hamlet chain across the country. I had the pleasure of decorating both of their penthouses, across the street from one another, and rather convenient for going back and forth. For whatever reasons, they kept separate residences. Marilyn was the most unusual and creative woman I had ever met. She was truly brilliant. Harry was handsome and a perfect gentleman—also a very smart businessman, especially friendly with his restaurant customers. We shared many dinner parties and traveling adventures across Europe and the Baltic.

We traveled on the *Crystal Symphony*, always first class, and had unforgettable times together. Marilyn and I loved to go shopping. We were both crazy and extravagant, especially in the '80s when money was so plentiful. Every Christmas, Marilyn would call me to go to the Neiman Marcus Christmas Party for their VIP clients. I picked her up and off we'd go. After all, this was my home away from home.

Marilyn Lewis

At one party, after a few cocktails, Marilyn began shopping. After making a few selections, she asked if she might borrow my NM credit card. I said, "Don't you have one?" She said no, further explaining that Harry had canceled her cards. She spent too much. So I said okay, knowing she would pay me back. Marilyn had done that on our travels to Europe. Harry controlled the money because Marilyn was terrible with it. I got used to her using my credit cards. After all, we were dear friends and remained so.

That evening, while coming

down the escalator, I see, in one of the glass showcases on the main floor, this gorgeous gold reclining cat with diamond eyes—not real diamonds. After we got Cristal, Orin and I pledged to buy a souvenir cat everywhere we traveled. We had an incredible collection.

I asked the saleslady, "Can I look at the cat?" From the locked case, she takes out the bejeweled cat and hands it to me. I was amazed. It was a gold Judith Leiber evening bag. It was so beautiful! Marilyn and I looked at each other with approval, and then I said, "I just have to have it." I asked the price. The saleslady opened the bag, took out the price tag, and responded, "Fifteen hundred dollars." I looked at her and said, "I'll take it!" It was a perfect new addition to our cat collection, and a Christmas present from me to me. It has been displayed prominently in our china cabinet in our last five homes—with the price tag still inside the bag. Today it would be triple the price.

After ten years in West Hollywood, I was again possessed with the urge to move. This time I was feeling uncomfortable even though we had a security system in our condo. My discomfort, in part, lay in the fact that we had to park our own cars in a street-level garage beneath our condo. It was possible that anyone with criminal intent could slip into the garage when the automatic gates opened. I was always looking back while entering and exiting our building.

My paranoia was justified by a robbery that took place years before at the Harper Avenue apartment. We only had one parking space in that garage. One late evening, having just come home from a fashion show I directed, with a trunk full of expensive Bob Mackie gowns and jewelry, Orin and I decided that I would take the single garage space and Orin would park on the street. As I exited the garage to keep an eye out for Orin's safety, two men jumped out of the nearby bushes, holding a gun to my head and demanding money. My gut reaction was to grab what I had in my pocket and throw it on the ground, saying, "Get the fuck out of here you son-of-a bitch!" Suddenly headlights and a blaring car horn were headed in my direction. It was Orin in his car. The two thugs made a hasty departure. I don't know if there were bullets in the gun!

The West Hollywood Police Department said I had reacted improperly—that I should not have resisted, just given them what they asked for. With my fancy car and abundance of jewelry, I was an easy target for potentially violent crime.

It was 1992. I was working on a commercial job for a client in Culver City, their executive offices. After leaving a meeting with my client, I passed a large shopping mall. I was not familiar with this area, but everyone knows I love shopping in new places. I drove into the parking lot of the Fox Hills Mall, got out of my Jaguar, and proceeded to see what was in this mall. It was late afternoon, so the mall wasn't crowded. I walked around and found a shoe store with a large selection of Italian shoes. They were also having a sale. I love sales of any kind.

After trying on several pairs of shoes, I looked up and noticed the salesmen watching the news on a small television set. The salesmen, who were helping me, were glued to the screen and I could hear lots of commotion coming from the TV. I asked what was going on. One salesman said that the verdict in the Rodney King case was about to be announced. He suggested that I should probably leave the mall in case there might be problems. I was not aware this mall catered to primarily African American customers. I suddenly felt scared and said, "I'll take these seven pair of shoes."

He said, "You want all of these?"

I replied, "Yes. You have a great selection." I handed him my American Express card and he proceeded to write up the transaction. However, the charge was over $1,000 so he had to call for authorization. Finally the salesman gets the okay. I grabbed the boxes and ran out of the mall.

People were gathered in the parking lot and talking excitedly. The verdict came back—acquittal! I immediately drove home. I turned on the TV to see the entire city in complete uproar over the verdict. The LA riots had begun. Thousands of protestors took to the streets, looting and burning businesses. The police had little or no control over the situation. I never went back to that mall.

I was very pleased with my shoes.

Shortly thereafter, we decided to move to a twenty-four-hour full security building in the premier condominium high-rise neighborhood known as the Wilshire Corridor in Westwood, not far from Orin's office at Twentieth Century Fox Studios. Orin did not put up any objections.

I contacted a realtor friend, Linda Faber, and she started looking for us. I knew I wanted to spend only half a million dollars. That was a lot of money to me and that's what she found.

A condo turned up on the fifteenth floor of the Regency Wilshire. The asking price was $569,000. It was a very elegant building on the North side of Wilshire, set a bit back off the boulevard. The lobby was attractive, plenty of granite and mirror—my look!

Unit 1501 had a grand foyer leading into a large living room with a built-in bar, dining room to the right and den to the left. The kitchen had a center island with a connecting breakfast room. Two bedrooms with walk-in closets and three baths completed the spacious layout. The floor-to-ceiling windows and balcony had spectacular views facing south as far as the Palos Verdes Peninsula.

"This is it," I told Orin. "Let's go for it." I made an offer of $500,000 and it was accepted, with a forty-five-day escrow.

We decided not to sell our beautiful condo in West Hollywood. We had witnessed a lot of history at this location. We had survived a big 6.1 earthquake in 1987 and the 1992 Los Angeles riots caused by the arrest and beating of Rodney King. I'll never forget watching the pockets of fire and destruction, as well as the approaching mobs, from our balcony. Fortunately the mayhem stopped within a short distance from our home.

No matter, I believed it would make a fine rental. It was located in a predominantly gay neighborhood within walking distance of virtually everything. We leased the unit to a lovely straight older couple. They had a gay son with AIDS who lived nearby and they wished to be close to him. They were wonderful tenants for many years.

Thus, I became a landlord, which I loved. My father had owned many properties and I'd learned a lot from him. We needed to remove several pieces of furniture and accessories to accommodate my new tenants. I decided to have a cocktail party–style estate sale. People were lined up at the door. It turned out to be a profitable endeavor while getting rid of years of accumulated furnishings that became treasures to the buyers.

I decided to give our new condo a very different look than the West Hollywood property. I wanted to go neoclassical, not contem-

porary, in color tones of coral, ivory, and black. It was a more traditional look. All my fabrics were from Scalamandre. I put in new marble baths, custom closets, and a marble slab entry floor. The unit had a guest powder room as well. I purchased an antique crystal chandelier for the dining room. What a showplace! It was very elegant and the perfect place for entertaining.

We were very proud of our new home on Wilshire Boulevard. We were movin' on up!

⚜20⚜

Hollywood Forever

By THIS TIME my work was being written up regularly in notable interior design publications, including the *LA Times*. Not to mention, I was having a good time socially. I was not so absent of mind or reality as to ignore my health. Every doctor I saw regarding my liver status kept repeating the same depressing commentary—STOP DRINKING!

I failed to listen, despite my foreknowledge of the danger ahead should such behavior not be altered immediately.

By nature, I'm the kind of person who tends to think ahead on practical matters, notwithstanding the drinking issue for which I lacked self-control. I recognized the severity of my health situation and did not wish to burden Orin with any fatal eventuality.

On this issue I resorted to cold logic. I began looking seriously at cemeteries, preparing for an ultimate repose that comes to all men. All the cemeteries resisted my demands to design my own memorial—or at least had strong reservations due to their strict building regulations and specifications. They would only allow a marker or small gravestone. I cared little for limitations and continued to pursue further options.

Then I remembered visiting a famous landmark cemetery in Hollywood, called aptly the Hollywood Memorial Park. Herein, lay for eternity the mortal remains of many famous film producers, legendary stars, and other luminaries who walked the corridors of Hollywood in decades past: director Cecil B. DeMille; actors Marion Davies, Mickey Rooney, and Judy Garland; and silent screen stars Rudolph Valentino and Douglas Fairbanks. The property boasted a beautiful lake, adorned with extraordinary white swans, fine trees, and rather fabulous marble monuments, some dating back almost a hundred years. It was everything I could possibly desire, and, again—so very Hollywood!

I did my onsite research by walking around the property and discovered a place by the lake that I liked immensely. It faced west, toward the ocean, and was next to film star Tyrone Power's burial place with a glorious view of the famous Hollywood Sign on the hill above the city itself. I went to the business office and decided to talk to Joe, who essentially ran the cemetery. When I mentioned the location I wished to solicit, he gave me a wry chuckle.

"Bernardo, that's prime property and it sold years ago," he said gently. "I can show you other spots, if you'd like, no less attractive."

"No, thank you." I sighed and held out my card. "If anything changes, please let me know."

As fate and my particular fortune would have it, a few months later, Joe gave me a call.

"Strangest thing happened, Bernardo. The people who owned those plots you liked so much, well, they're moving to Chicago and wish to sell their property."

He sounded genuinely surprised, but I wasn't at all. If I wanted something badly enough . . . I got it. I told Joe I'd take the property and be in the next day with the money.

That's how I got my plots at Hollywood Memorial Park.

Years passed. The cemetery fell into disrepair and was on the brink of closure. The endowment fund, meant to care for the cemetery in perpetuity, was missing a small fortune. Hollywood Memorial Park was purchased in a bankruptcy proceeding by the current owner, Tyler Cassity. He took over quickly and dropped millions to beautify his new cemetery, going so far as to rename the place Hollywood Forever Cemetery. I'm, of course, thrilled by the change and renovation. Tyler and I became friends and he helped with the design and construction of our monument.

In addition to cemetery duty, it also fell upon me to plan and design my fiftieth birthday extravaganza. I researched the perfect venue that might accommodate 250 guests and decided on the Beverly Wilshire Hotel. I then booked Le Grand Trianon for dinner and Le Petite Trianon for a pre-dinner cocktail party. Since it was my fiftieth (and fifty is golden), I decided to adorn the entire ballroom in, what else, black and gold. Very chic and my favorite colors.

I designed the invitation with Lehr and Black, owners Sol and Ellen being my favorite go-to printing people for years. Their mother, Marsha, who had worked with me before, came out of retirement to work on my invitations, and she did an incredible job.

So now we had our location, the date, and the invitations. Three main items remained. We hired the Bob Gail Orchestra. They were very popular and came with an entire package—expensive, but worth it. We were able to procure the stars of the national company of *Phantom of the Opera* to perform. Ruta Lee, our dear friend, agreed to entertain.

Keeping with the theme, the table settings and décor were black and gold. Only the flowers were white with gold leaves in gold vases. The ballroom was magnificent! My name was spelled out in lights against a gold rain curtain.

Fifty was an important, symbolic year for me. I was at the height of my career; my social life was simply magical. I'll never forget two special Birmingham guests. My sister Sarah and her daughter Liz surprised me by attending. Not only did they share my special birthday with me, they also got to experience my lifestyle in Los Angeles, which meant so much to me.

To this day, I have people who attended this significant event come up to me and say that they would never forget Bernardo's fiftieth birthday party. Neither will I. What an expensive event—it was worth every penny.

What an incredible evening!

Ruta Lee and Webb Lowe

⊰ 21 ⊱

From Here, to There, Now Where?

Aᴼᶠᵀᴱᴿ ꜰɪᴠᴇ ʏᴇᴀʀꜱ, in 1996, Orin and I decided the time was right to sell the Regency Wilshire condo, take our profit, and continue upsizing. Our desire was to remain on the Wilshire Corridor. We found a magnificent place at a great price, on the next block, at the exclusive Wilshire House. We were in a double escrow to sell and buy when suddenly we were faced with a traumatic situation.

No problem with the sale, but as it turned out, the rules at the Wilshire House had a small but devastating paragraph that we failed to notice, nor had it been pointed out to us by anyone. Said clause stated a homeowner living in the building had the first right to buy the same unit. All they had to do was meet the price we had negotiated. I had never heard of such a provision. And so it happened that a realtor living in the building, realizing we had negotiated a great deal, elected to select that option. We were defenseless and mad as hell. And this was just two weeks before we were scheduled to move.

Plans had been drawn, estimates to remodel in place, and now we had nowhere to go! What do we do? That was the question! The only answer at the time—put our belongings into storage and move into a hotel, cat and all!

We were fortunate to find a one-bedroom suite, fully furnished down to linens and dishware, with a kitchenette at the nearby Beverly Hills Plaza Hotel where we could stay until we found a permanent residence. Within a week we located and bought our next home at the Diplomat. Yes, on Wilshire Boulevard again and next door to our hotel.

It was a spacious three-thousand-square-foot condo on the seventeenth floor with an absolutely breathtaking view of the city. One plus factor was we didn't have far to go to supervise, yes, the renovation. Unfortunately, we had no time to haggle, under the circumstances, and we had to pay the asking price. We closed escrow in no time and prepared to remodel. Two months later we moved into our new home. Orin loved living at the hotel with its charming restaurant and daily maid service. Cristal was contented too.

We resided at the Diplomat for three years, long enough to take whatever profit there might be as a tax-free deduction upon the sale. Even with the fantastic views and space, the place felt cold. It never possessed the warmth of a home for the keeping. I had bought it as an investment to redo and sell. That was eventually what I did. So, while we had enjoyed many dinner parties, with great themes and food ranging from Italian to Moroccan to Egyptian, this was never going to be my permanent dream home, if indeed there was such a place. So on the market it went and within a few weeks it sold. Now, where to?

From our sky-high balcony, Orin had always admired a mid-century twelve-story building whose residents were mostly older and wealthy. It was situated three blocks around the corner on Beverly Glen Boulevard.

As fate would have it, one day, we received a phone call from a realtor friend, Susan Marks. She had heard that Orin and I were in the market to buy a new place. I wanted to keep the price of any prospects within the $500,000 range, preferably less. Susan said the condo she had in mind was not on the market as yet. The owners had passed away a few years earlier. However, the family secretary and her two kids were living there, and according to Susan, the place desperately needed the Puccio touch.

I was intrigued. So the next day, Orin and I went to see the condo. To say the place was a mess would be a major understatement. Not surprising, really—a single mother who had been the secretary of the deceased owner, with two little girls and two cats, was temporarily residing in the unit. I, of course, was vocal in my displeasure—a common buying strategy to show indifference. But, in truth, I saw great promise in the place. It included a large entry hall, a great living and dining room combination, and a kitchen with a breakfast room that looked out onto a very large balcony that ran the whole length of the unit. What really sold me was the million-dollar view that each room looked out to—an unobstructed southern view of downtown LA, Century City, and the Pacific Ocean. I considered this asset nothing short of magical. I could make this a showplace!

Orin and I returned home and decided to go for it! We were accustomed to a full-service building and the condo in question provided this as well. I called the realtor the next day and requested a second look but with the caveat that it be cleaned ahead of time, excised of cat feces and other offensive debris. I also asked to see the place at night. By God, when I walked in at dusk, all the lights were glistening throughout the city. The view was truly awe-inspiring.

To our surprise, the realtor informed us that the unit came with what was called a separate maid's unit on the ground floor, basically a studio apartment with bath. After showing us this additional feature, I was convinced this was for us. It was all too good to be true. The purchase price was stated and I accepted it without hesitation—as is, with a ten-day escrow. My instructions to the mother: Do nothing with the place—that would be my job. Just take the money and get out ASAP—young mother, her kids, and her cats.

Dealing with these negotiations and my design business was extremely stressful. I found myself socializing and drinking to take the edge off. Often, I would stay up until the early hours of the morning. This is when I did most of my best design work. In total silence with no phone calls, my brain could be devoted exclusively to the creative process.

The entire condo needed complete renovation along with the separate guest quarters. Orin usually agreed with my creative choices when it came to the interior design of our homes. We once again took up residence at the Beverly Hills Plaza Hotel, along with Cristal. He adapted, except when it came to housekeeper visitations and the vacuum cleaner. Those he could not tolerate!

Every morning for two months, I opened up the condo for the workers. I would then stay and oversee daily operations, finally locking up at 6:00 p.m. Once renovation was completed, we all moved in. It was a time-consuming endeavor, but necessary, as I wanted to alter the 1960 straight-line modern architecture.

In its place I planned a more traditional neoclassical design with curved arches, crown molding, wood flooring, Venetian plaster walls, magnificent drapery, and of course, the most gorgeous furnishings I could lay my hands on. I chose to use colors of gold and black, with an accent of red. A very dramatic Italian villa décor was the result. I loved it. It took two months of constant work, the finest craftsmen available, and my ever-persevering eye—but it all proved worth it. Luxurious.

We finally moved in with intentions that this would be our final home where we'd live out our lives. Well, for myself, I held some private reservations. Nevertheless, we enjoyed the building and met some very neighborly people who lived there. I felt the building was old and could definitely use a facelift.

Orin, meanwhile, joined the Board of Directors, on my suggestion, and became vice president, while our pal, Hal Taines, was the president. Hal was an old client of mine. He and his wife, Sue, lived in the building for thirty years. Hal was quite the wheeler-dealer, which had made him a multimillionaire. His business interests ran the gamut of hotelier in Miami Beach, oil wells in Oklahoma, and motion picture production. He attended the Cannes Film Festival for years. He was a real-life Damon Runyon character.

Not long after, an accidental fire occurred in the garbage chute and the resulting smoke traversed several floors, causing extensive damage. Hal went to work and after several months of negotiating, he got the insurance company to provide the building with a million dollars for renovation. The board interviewed three designers, but of course, I got the job. It took six months of assiduous work to remodel and decorate. I used only the finest design elements, enhancing the lobby with black granite flooring, a luxurious custom designed area rug, new furniture, fabrics, wall coverings, accessories, and a grand contemporary crystal chandelier. My colors of choice ranged from beige to taupe, accented with turquoise. The ultimate touch was, of course, a touch of black.

The enterprise turned out to be a stunning success. What a difference. Lobby, elevators, corridors were all refurbished. In addition, I insisted on repainting the exterior of the building, all twelve stories. We even installed a new driveway. Final touches included fresh orchids . . . of course.

This had been a Puccio signature project. Homeowners and visitors, for many years to come, would see the results of my talent. I looked at this building as a part of my immortality—and that remarkable bookmarked marble wall I'd created in the lobby would last until the apocalypse.

We used our ground-floor maid's unit, which consisted of one room and bath with its own private entrance, as a guest unit. It was a great place for out-of-town guests and extra storage. Many friends stayed there and enjoyed their privacy, in particular, our good friend, Bill Mathay, who lived in Hollywood, Florida.

Bill was a kind and gentle older man. A retired hairdresser, he loved to travel. We met him on our first European cruise, from Venice to Barcelona, coordinated by the Thalians charitable organization. Bill loved Hollywood and film stars. He was possessed with getting their autographs and even carried eight-by-ten photos he had taken or bought over the years, for them to sign. Everywhere we went, Bill would stalk out and find celebrities. He had an incredible collection of signed photos in his Florida home. We enjoyed Bill's company, whether in Florida or when he came to Los Angeles. I never minded him staying in our guest unit. He came and went as he wanted, and we got together when it was convenient.

Every Friday we had lunch at the Bistro Gardens, which catered to high society and the film industry, knowing Bill would get to see some celebrities. On this particular Friday, Bill spotted Nancy Reagan, lunching with her lady friends. Bill quickly made his way over to her as she was leaving to ask for her autograph. Nancy was pleasant and obliged.

The following Friday at the Bistro Gardens, Bill once again spotted Mrs. Reagan. He approached her, this time outside in front of the restaurant's entrance, and asked if she would consent to take a photograph with him. I assumed she did. However, something must have bothered Mrs. Reagan or her Secret Service escort.

When I came home that afternoon, the manager of our building called and asked if I had a houseguest staying with me from Florida.

I said, "Yes, but why are you asking?"

She replied, "Because the Reagans' Secret Service came to our building to investigate if your houseguest was legitimate."

This was right after 9/11 and security was extra tight. I was shocked and upset about this entire ordeal. I believe everyone has the right to privacy. When Bill returned, later that afternoon, I told him what had transpired and how upset I was. What was so strange—how did the Secret Service track Bill to my address? The only thing I could figure out was that when Bill rented a car at the airport, he must have given the rental company my address as his destination. And that was how they traced him to me. I asked Bill to, please, never do that again. Bill was a dear friend and we miss his visits, but not those of the Secret Service.

❧22❧

Celebration of Life

I𝖳'𝗌 2004. I'𝗆 sick as hell and getting sicker by the day. My liver is giving out due to the abuse I levied against it through the years. Numerous doctors had already conveyed to me that, without a transplant, I wouldn't see next year. I had resisted their sage advice. At the time, I sincerely believed I could just weather out my health condition with typical Puccio resolve. If it was time for me to die and God was calling me home—so be it. Up to this point, I'd shared with no one, not even Orin, the seriousness of my liver disease. I'd kept this dire fact secret.

According to my nature, I could not resist the temptation to plan ahead. I explained to Orin that it was a good idea to simply move forward and erect our memorial on the property I'd bought years ago at the Hollywood Forever Cemetery, the final resting place to so many stars and celebrities of years past. Orin was surprisingly in accord with my suggestion. I began to design my monument. Not just any monument, to be sure.

I met with an architect and conveyed my building specifications. The plans were astounding: a magnificent twelve-foot-high

Greco-Roman marble monument that was situated lakeside, facing west and toward the Hollywood Sign. Orin and I were joyfully overwhelmed with the result. Along with both of our names engraved atop the monument, I added Cristal's name at the base of the urn that would eventually hold all our ashes.

The monument was completed two years later in 2006. As always, I wanted something more. A young man, Jay Gianukos, whom the cemetery had hired to create videos for the families of the deceased, followed us for nearly a year, filming highlights of our life, including a trip to my hometown—Birmingham, Alabama. The videos, a gift from cemetery owner Tyler Cassity, were to be shown at the respective funeral services. As always, I wanted something more. I felt it only appropriate to throw a party!

After the video was completed, invitations went out which read:

You are selectively invited to attend a very special event to honor the longtime partnership of Bernardo Puccio and Orin Kennedy at the dedication of their monument and red carpet premiere of the personal documentary Two Hearts Two Souls... Lakeside in the Garden of Legends, Hollywood Forever.

No one declined the invite. Everyone had a sense of curiosity about what Orin and I were up to this time. Why were they having a party at a cemetery? Fact is, some guests didn't even associate our invitation's location with a cemetery. One couple, reading "Hollywood Forever," thought they were going to a garden party in some new place. It was also coincidental that West Hollywood's Gay Pride Parade was happening at the same time.

On a late afternoon in June, over a hundred friends and family gathered for cocktails and hors d'oeuvres at Hollywood Forever Cemetery under a large tent. My sister Marietta and her husband flew in from Birmingham for the occasion. After an hour of greetings, we all retired to the cemetery's Cathedral Mausoleum. Orin stood and gave a brief welcoming speech and then introduced me. I said that a short video would be shown, celebrating our life together. When the video ended, the crowd stood and applauded for several minutes. Seeing our intertwining life and love story unfold on the screen through narration, photos, and video proved to be a moving experience for us both.

We then all assembled outside at our monument site, which was draped in white silk, adorned with purple and white flowers.

I had hired an opera singer to help set the mood. Orin and I stood, side by side, explaining the true purpose of this Celebration of Life—to unveil our monument as a testament that Puccio and Kennedy shared a beautiful life together.

On the monument was inscribed the following:

TWO HEARTS, TWO LIVES

TOGETHER IN LIFE

FOREVER IN ETERNITY

Again, the applause was overwhelming. I was told our attorney Ada Sands said, "I came here with an attitude. What the hell is happening? Why are we here?" She then responded to her own questions: "It turned out to be an incredible experience, with a lot of introspection. It transformed me."

Fashion icon Mr. Blackwell said, "It was a lesson in love and understanding. I wish we had more of it."

Philanthropist Joyce Black said, "This has been one of the most memorable days of my life."

Local news anchor and novelist Kelly Lange revealed she wasn't sure what to make of the whole experience!

As the sun began to set, all the guests, members of the press, and photographers admitted to us they had an unexpected and emotionally moving afternoon the likes of which they'd never experienced. It proved to be such a unique event that we were featured on the front page of the *Los Angeles Times* Calendar section the following Sunday.

The *LA Times* headline read: *In death they do not part—in fact, they have a party.* Robin Abcarian wrote, "It provoked scattered tears and knowing laughs." The article was transmitted worldwide.

Orin and I were overwhelmed by the reception.

Back home, we capped off the evening entertaining a small group of close friends, and recapturing this special day. As guests arrived,

Cristal, our still beautiful, though senior cat, assumed a royal position in his favorite chair, where he remained for the duration of the occasion. As people began to leave, only then would he dismiss himself and go about his business.

Shortly thereafter, Cristal started to have problems associated with his age. He was almost eighteen years old and for the past year we knew his kidneys were failing, but he was still eating. The vet suggested we supplement his diet with daily fluids, which required intravenous injections under the skin. Not a pleasant procedure for any of us. This routine went on for a year. Cristal was less and less inclined to eat food or drink water. He even stopped grooming himself, and I could tell by looking at his coat something was seriously wrong. We did everything to make him comfortable.

One night, I heard an unexpected yelp coming from the bathroom—a cry of distress. Cristal was crouched with his back toward his food and water bowls. The food hadn't been touched. Most alarming, he wasn't able to stand. I realized the inevitable had finally arrived. I tearfully put Cristal into his carrying case and we drove to the vet, still hoping that she could do something to save, even prolong his life. Having had experience previously with Orin's two cats, I feared the end was near. Orin and I had promised we would not let Cristal suffer. The time had come.

The vet examined Cristal and looked to Orin and me. "You did the right thing by bringing him in," she told us gently. "It's time to let him go." There was nothing more she could do.

I could say nothing. I was dying inside. This was truly the most difficult decision we had to make.

We were led to a private room for the procedure that would end Cristal's physical existence in this life. I held him in my arms, stroking him, saying how much we loved him. Orin sat across from us staring at Cristal's face for the last time. I can't remember ever crying like that before—nor had I ever seen Orin weep. The vet assured us that Cristal would receive a single injection and would feel no pain. He would simply go to sleep.

Orin left the room and I said my private goodbyes.

To this day we think of Cristal—our little white prince. Pet lovers like to believe there is a Rainbow Bridge a pet crosses over. I feel he is in Pet Heaven, having a wonderful time.

He is dearly remembered and missed to this very day.

⊰23⊱

Greystone

OUR LIVES WERE filled with work, travel abroad, and a never-ending social life of parties and charity events. We had our share of tragedy during the '80s and '90s with the loss of parents, friends, and siblings. Both of Orin's sisters and my sister Sarah succumbed to cancer, all at an early age.

Orin was a middle child of three. There was a five-year difference in age between them. From the time he was seventeen, Orin's family accepted his being gay. His younger sister, Leslie, had found his diary and brought it to their parents, thinking "Danny"—Orin's birth name—was sick. She was only twelve years old. Their mother, who had sensed Orin was going through some sort of change, brought him to her psychiatrist, hoping for an answer. After one session, the doctor declared to Orin's parents, "You have two choices. Either accept him for who he is, or ask him to leave home." Need I say more? Orin came from a close family. The decision was obvious. Over the years I connected with Orin's whole family and was treated with great respect and love as his partner.

Orin's older sister, Harlene, after a two-year struggle with colon cancer, succumbed to the disease in 1981 at the age of forty-eight. Before passing, she admitted to Orin that, although she accepted his being gay, it was difficult for her to accept her older son William's coming out. Interesting to note both Harlene's sons were gay; the eldest, William, died of AIDS in 1994, after his mother's passing. The very same year, Orin's younger sister, Leslie, passed away suddenly at fifty, from the side effects of chemotherapy for breast cancer. This happened on the day of her daughter's wedding. How we managed those tragedies was a testament to our love.

My sister Sarah suffered for over two years going through chemotherapy and losing her beautiful hair. It was a devastating situation for her daughters Liz and Margie. There were happy years prior. Sarah got to see them graduate college, marry, and have children of their own, whom she adored. In 2001, I lost my sister and best friend at age sixty-eight. She knew my first partner, Jim, and had gotten close with Orin, both of whom she loved. She was a sensitive person, a devoted mother and grandmother. I will always remember Sarah, our lunches, shopping, going to the movies, and just enjoying each other's company. I was devastated at her passing.

Following twenty-seven years as a successful location manager for the film studios, Orin decided to retire in 2004. I couldn't blame him—he'd put in his time. Reality had also set in. My health was deteriorating and Orin really wanted to devote his time to me. Orin had always been such a loving caregiver, though the greater extent of his promise in this endeavor would not be fully realized until later.

I had made a lot of money during my career and was now at a stage where I could be selective, thank God. One day, I received a call from a friend of mine who was on the Board of the American Society of Interior Designers.

"Bernardo," he said, "we have a Designer Show House coming up and we'd like you to do a room at Greystone Mansion. This is not a request—we need your touch. We need your name for this particular showcase! Please don't say no!"

Well, I'd never done anything like this before, nor was I particularly enthusiastic to take on such an assignment now. I was feeling sick and losing focus, but did not wish to explain my health situation to anyone. I was slowing down—I looked like hell, I felt worse. I said, "Okay."

Built in the late 1920s, Greystone Mansion and Gardens was the former Doheny estate located in Beverly Hills. The family had made their fortune in oil. The property was eventually purchased by the City of Beverly Hills and became a historic landmark. One room in particular, the Solarium, was well lit with natural light, limestone floors, and walls. I decided this was the room I would tackle.

It took about three weeks to complete this eclectic design within the room's grandiose architecture. I used antiques, Lucite furniture, and some fabulous furnishings from my own private collection. I was very proud of my achievement. This room, in particular, received lots of publicity and recognition. However, I was not feeling well and was finding it more difficult to make my way uphill from the parking lot to the residence, let alone stand for any length of time. Orin came to the rescue and hosted the room tours for the week.

I really didn't think I'd acquire any business from doing the aforementioned project, but as it turned out, this enterprise yielded quite another kind of reward—that of a young European woman wishing to buy my Lucite chairs at an exceptional price.

A special show house tour was arranged for twenty-four of my "Beverly Hills ladies"—friends and clients. After the showing, I took them all to lunch at Morton's, home to Vanity Fair's Oscar parties, in West Hollywood. I always enjoyed entertaining the ladies in style. My illness had progressed. Everyone knew it, but had the courtesy not to say anything.

The good times continued even as my health progressively declined.

❧ 24 ❧

The Wedding

ON MAY 15, 2008, the California Supreme Court struck down two state laws that had limited marriages to unions between a man and a woman, and ruled that same-sex couples had a constitutional right to marry. Same-sex marriage became legal in California. At sixty-four years old, I had never imagined I would see this historic day during my lifetime. Yet here it was. As usual, for Orin and me, the timing was perfect.

In 1952 when I played with my mother's wedding dress, merely a toy for me at the time, I could never have dreamed that it might end up serving as a kind of metaphor for a life well imagined and lived. Every dream I had ever hoped for had come true, and then some. By October 12, 2008, another dream was to be realized.

Orin and I would be legally married. We decided, with the encouragement of our friends Beverly and Bob Cohen, that our wedding would be held at the Four Seasons Los Angeles at Beverly Hills Hotel, which the Cohens owned.

To think this momentous celebration was happening because of an unexpected California court ruling was absolutely mind-boggling.

The details were all coming together nicely for what I imagined would be the "gay" wedding of the century: guest list, invitations, wedding party, photographer, videographer, and officiant.

As the days counted down, I was still in the throes of wedding event planning. I wasn't prepared for the overwhelming anxiety that would eventually hit me when the actual day managed to sneak up on me.

On the morning of our wedding, I was admittedly nervous, though I endeavored to put on a stoic air. My wedding day had arrived at first without much fanfare. I don't think it had sunk in yet. Orin and I had begun all the planning mere weeks after the court ruling. Now it was just hours away. Orin was fairly emotional with commingled joy and anxiety. For me, I was still taking care of business.

Orin began to have butterflies. I'd sit quietly for a respite on the sidelines while dozens of workers feverishly attended to the details. In those thoughtful times, it crossed my mind how strange and wonderful life could be. After planning so many events for various individuals throughout my career, including weddings, it never occurred to me that I'd be celebrating my own nuptials one day.

My life to this point had been an extraordinary journey. So maybe it shouldn't have been such a surprise to me after all. I was the same Bernardo Puccio who had traveled the world and dined with Hollywood royalty, the same Bernardo who had flown in a Cessna jet cross-country just to meet friends for dinner. The same man who pushed a check back across the table to one Mable Taber in favor of a life of freedom. So should it then be such a shock that I would also be among the wave of the first gay couples to marry that year in California?

No. Not at all.

As with any project that carried the Puccio stamp, my wedding not only would be exquisite, but I decided it would be the most notable event I had ever planned. Love is in the details, as the saying goes. My wedding was no exception. From the gold floral beaded tablecloths to the wedding party's turquoise gowns and black tuxedos with matching turquoise ties, every detail was planned to perfection. The floral arrangements composed of white orchids and lilies were everywhere. I hired Kevin Lee of LA Premier, the most fabulous florist in all of California. We invited 250 people from all corners of the country and not one person declined the invitation. Orin's cousins came from New Jersey and Florida. Our friends, many of whom we met on our travels, flew in from New York, Massachusetts, and Texas. There were seven states represented at the party. I thought to myself, Bernardo, you've got to let go. The event will be beautiful. Let go and enjoy. I managed to let go, if not silently, doing a mental checklist in my mind. Still, as the moment drew closer, I began to ponder the "how" of it all.

Six p.m. was approaching quickly. I thought back to the day I met Orin at the Garden District, how elegant and polite he had been. I thought of a recent toast he had made to me: "Thank you for making my home a palace and my life a fairy tale." If I were to echo that sentiment, I might have responded: "Thank you for sharing your life with me and for showing me what real love is!" I didn't say that, of course.

As I stood in the wedding party waiting room, everything suddenly became very real. Orin was nervous. I was more reflective. We had realized so many dreams together. I remember thinking how, only a short time earlier we hosted a Celebration of Life event at Hollywood Forever Cemetery. Many people compared that occasion to a wedding. In a way, so did I. During a TV interview at the time, when asked about the grandeur of the event and its comparison to a wedding, I remarked, "Well, it's as close to a wedding as we'll ever get."

I never could have imagined what was about to happen.

The music began—the traditional Bach's Air on the G String. The procession commenced with the groomsmaids, groomsmen, and friends. The Alabama contingent included my niece Carrie, her brother Paul, and his wife, Katie, and our girlfriend Deborah

Goldstein was there from Dallas. Orin followed nervously, as if being physically supported, with his best friends Carole and Alice. Finally it was my turn. Arm in arm with my sister Marietta, I slowly made my way down the aisle, blowing kisses to the gathered guests who returned the affection with a standing ovation.

Wedding Party

A dear friend, Los Angeles Councilman Bill Rosendahl, officiated the wedding vows. And then it was over. I turned to our friends and family and threw them all a kiss.

"We're married!" I yelled out and was greeted with laughter and a standing applause. I looked to Orin, who had tears in his eyes.

We entered the grand ballroom to the live music of Bobby Rivas and commenced the first dance to another round of standing applause. In that moment everything became unreal as if we were dancing on a cloud. The clapping was motion, not a sound. It was just the two of us, in each other's arms. After a very long engagement, we were finally a married couple.

The evening continued with toasts from Gloria Allred, Bill Rosendahl, Marietta, Carole, and Alice. Actress Ruta Lee and Helen Grayco both sang songs with heartfelt lyrics in our honor. The last thing I remember, after the guests had left, was dancing in the soft glow of the ballroom with Orin in my arms, reflecting on this unbelievable evening and the past thirty-two years.

Gloria Allred

We'd done it! We were married, a historic day to be sure, although things were about to take a shocking turn.

Just three weeks later, on November 4, 2008, a measure to ban gay marriage in California—Proposition 8—was approved by voters, throwing into doubt our marriage and the unions of an estimated eighteen thousand same-sex couples who had wed during the last five and a half months. We were thrown into a no-man's land.

However, six months later the California Supreme Court ruled, while upholding the gay marriage ban, that gay couples who wed before the election, which included us, would continue to be married under state law.

For the next seven years marriage equality went back and forth through the court system. In a final victory for the gay rights movement, on June 26, 2015, the United States Supreme Court ruled that the Constitution guaranteed a right to same-sex marriage to all citizens.

⫷25⫸

The Transplant

Eᴀʀʟɪᴇʀ ɪɴ 2008, two years after the Hollywood Forever screening event, I had received a call from Jay Gianukos, the videographer, expressing his desire to make a feature-length documentary out of the original life story video *Two Hearts, Two Souls* by expanding the story. As I was becoming progressively sicker, I had no interest.

"I'm not doing well," I said to Orin. "The last thing I want is to be filmed looking like hell." By this time my complexion had taken on a jaundiced appearance. Thank God for makeup!

I rarely could deny Orin anything he felt strongly about. He was enthusiastic about the idea, so I said, "Go ahead."

My health continued to deteriorate. On the last night of principal photography, I invited a few close friends over to watch the presidential election night results. My mental state was undergoing significant biological changes brought about by my altered physical condition, which was beyond my control. I became so ill that it became necessary to ask Jay to suspend any further filming and leave my home. Our friends had fortunately left by this time after watching President

Obama give his election night acceptance speech. I confessed to Orin how sick I felt. It was now the end of 2008 and I was at death's door.

As far as I was concerned, filming was finished, and editing began. Jay had chosen to bring a young woman, Susan Barnes, on to the project as editor and co-director. She spent months cutting the documentary, now titled *An Ordinary Couple*. Orin and I never felt comfortable with the title. People with whom we discussed it were confused and remarked that our life story and personalities were anything but ordinary.

"Extraordinary!" was the word they used, but Jay and Susan were absolutely convinced their title was appropriate for the storyline. We reluctantly acquiesced.

I'll never forget going to a recording session in Hollywood with the whole crew where we viewed the completed film for the first time along with a compelling, original music score written by composer Bronwen Jones. It was really happening!

My health by late September 2009 had deteriorated to such a point where some mornings I did not recognize my reflection in the mirror. It was becoming clearer with each passing day that my illness had escalated to a daily ordeal of pain and debilitation. I was weaker; my energy had all but abandoned me.

I set up an appointment with a young doctor from Cedars-Sinai Hospital who specialized in liver disease. After he reviewed my medical records, he flatly declared I would not see Christmas if I did not immediately stop drinking. I was so shocked by his rude declaration, I responded with Sicilian ire: "You know, doctor, your bedside manner sucks. You have no idea how to deal with sick patients. Furthermore, you send me a bill and I'll toss it in the garbage where you belong!"

Of course, it was an irrational response on my part, but the young asshole had pissed me off. He never did send me an invoice. I did not believe he would. As I walked out of the hospital, I summarized three possible options for my life in the near future: 1) I could drive myself off the nearest cliff and end this bullshit completely; 2) I could head for the nearest bar and drink myself silly; or 3) I could simply go home, stop drinking, have the transplant, and hopefully live a somewhat normal life from then on.

I chose this last option.

And this is where the nightmare really begins.

My sixty-sixth birthday was not exactly celebratory in nature. It was spent in the hospital surrounded by very able doctors and kind nurses. I was at stage five, otherwise known as end-stage liver disease. I had finally made the decision to go through with the liver transplant and thus my team was in NASA-like readiness to evaluate and launch.

I was to be subjected to a plethora of tests to determine my body's ability to accept an alien liver, but also to discern if I was physiologically and psychologically up to this most serious surgical procedure.

I, as well as everyone around me, knew how advanced my cirrhosis had become. I was oddly prepared for this part of the nightmare, but I was ill prepared for the military-like assault on my body with constant needles poking me at any given minute. Thank God and the angels' grace that I could slip into unconsciousness periodically and escape the insanity. Those little slices of death were a welcome distraction from the ongoing and incessant pre-surgical physical evaluation. Every so often, I'd hear someone mutter "Happy birthday" to me. How farcical and surreal that seems to me now.

After a full day of this invasive prodding, Dr. Woolf, my chief physician, told me I could go home. Yay. Happy birthday, Bernardo! Orin was understandably more exhausted than I, as he had consciously remained with me throughout this endless day of exams.

We waited at home for the results, which were due within a few days. Finally, the good doctor called.

"Bernardo, apart from your liver, you're in fine physical condition," he said in an optimistic tone of voice. I chuckled inwardly. That's like saying, "Well, besides *that*, Mrs. Kennedy, how was Dallas?"

"Thank you, doctor," I whispered back into the phone. "What next?"

"You've been placed on a donor waiting list," he said solemnly.

Soon enough, my illness had progressed to the point where it was absolutely necessary that I be admitted to the hospital. My kidneys began to fail. I was dying.

The doctors immediately put me on dialysis, an ordeal I would not wish upon my worst enemy. Fluids were pumped into me to restore some functionality to my kidneys. Good luck. I was failing fast. Orin, God bless him, stayed by my side throughout the grueling ordeal. I periodically insisted he go home to shower and rest. It was hard for him and in a few days my concern truly empathized with Orin's condition—I was genuinely worried for his health.

I estimated rather coolly that I had a few days left. That was an optimistic projection to be sure. A Catholic priest was called in and I was administered the traditional last rites. I thought, This is it, *adios muchachos, vaya con dios*. Welcome to Eternity.

I was in the hospital for approximately two weeks, still on the fucking dialysis machine, at which point I made the organ transplant waiting list. Because of my grave condition, I went right to the top. Time was not on my side!

A liver became available. I was prepped for surgery as the liver entered the first phase of evaluation to determine if it was a match with my body. It turned out not to be a viable match—disappointing.

We continued to wait as I slipped closer to the abyss. Orin, my Florence Nightingale, stayed close for it all, watching the doctors and nurses like a predatory chicken hawk, making sure no one screwed up with my care.

The next day, a second liver arrived. Again I was prepped but it, too, was not a match—devastating. I never gave up and kept my belief in God.

On the third day another liver arrived and I was once again prepped. We all prayed as this latest liver arrival was assessed.

It was a match!

Preparation for surgery was made immediately. As I was wheeled into the operating room, numerous memories filled my mind: nostalgic talks with my mother in the kitchen, enchanting days in Europe, and my loving years with Orin. These little moments of retrospection were intermingled with the very real impending moment—and a fierce determination to survive this current odyssey.

My body was in crisis mode, attacked by an enemy I could not defeat on my own, yet my mind and spirit were still ready for combat. The surgery, I was told, would begin within minutes. This was the loneliest moment of my life. I suppose dying is a lonely business for us all—and ultimately inevitable. The battle into the unknown is a solitary one with no lifeline to call.

There is a truism to the near-death experience, perhaps for all of us when that dramatic day arrives: The looming question of whether we wish to go on living, to perpetuate the fight, becomes monolithic in breadth and scope. Do you wish to live? Are you ready to make that decision now? Unless paralysis has fully taken over your will and faculties, the natural human reaction is one of survival. Yes, I'm ready to fight now, a little while longer. Yes, I still choose life. Not today, please God, not today.

The cerebral and practical decision-making process had passed. I'd put my affairs in order. Everything had been put in place. I was ready to go to war.

"All right, Bernardo," the anesthesiologist said to me quietly. "Are you ready to go?"

I looked at him, his face a hazy blur. I'm not sure that I even nodded affirmatively, but he said: "Very good. Sit back and enjoy the ride."

The surgery lasted twelve hours.

I wish I could say I had visions of heaven during that time under anesthesia. In truth, I experienced only a blissful darkness, which from my perception lasted only a few minutes. I was later to learn from Orin that the surgeon had informed him, "Bernardo received

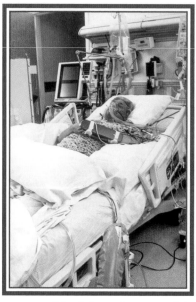

a beautiful, pink, healthy liver. He is being wheeled into ICU and is doing well."

When I awoke the following morning, I saw Orin standing at the foot of the hospital bed. He later related to me that with outstretched arms I screamed out, "My husband! I love you!" I was probably so doped up that my declaration came out of nowhere. I was never predisposed to such emotional outcries, but at that moment I was so happy to see Orin that my customary behavior was thrown by the wayside. More than anything else, I was ecstatic to still be alive.

The days and months of illness leading up to my transplant, the pre-op, and the surgery were one part of a nightmare, but nothing could prepare me for the period of recovery. I will not mince words—it was simply fucking brutal.

Three months of home care. Visiting nurses came every few days to check the incision, which ran the width of my body, and change bandages. I visited Cedars weekly for bloodwork, to monitor my progress, and to make sure there were no signs of rejection. Every time self-pity attempted to take over, I simply told myself, rather caustically: "Come on, Bernardo, this is the easy part. You made it through hell and back. You'd kicked the Devil in the balls and lived to tell about it—you got through the worst."

The adjustment in lifestyle was likewise difficult. I was now taking dozens of anti-rejection drugs every day, a practice I was informed I would have to do, hopefully in lesser amounts, for the rest of my life. Orin was there for me through it all. We had enjoyed the presence of a private nurse for one day, but after an unfortunate car accident, she never returned. Orin took over. To be sure, I drove him nuts much of the time, but he never faltered. After another three months, I was to face physical therapy. As difficult as this phase admittedly was, I began to feel like my old self again. No. Much better. I'd lost thirty-five pounds, much of it water weight, due to my illness. Still, I was weak and frail.

Writing this particular chapter is both agonizing and cathartic. My willingness to relive this darkest of my days did not come easily to me. The only way I've been able to revisit these horrible times has been to put myself into a literal semiconscious trance. Trauma is not easy to reconstitute, even if only through the written word. I write this in large part to hopefully help others who are now going through what I experienced to find the courage to live and make correct decisions that will help you, your friends, and family.

I continue to thank God for Orin, family, and friends who prayed for me through my surgery. Most especially I thank the organ donor.

God had heard their prayers—and mine.

For this I am eternally grateful.

Wherever you are, whoever you may be, I thank you daily from the bottom of my heart. To the entire Liver Clinic at Cedars-Sinai, I thank you most profoundly. You, dear doctors and nurses of that sublime department, are part of my miracle. For without you, I would not be here today.

Thank you for the miracle of life!

During my recovery from the transplant, I asked my doctor if I might attend a gathering of friends. Our friend, Gail Dauer, was having a party to introduce her twin baby granddaughters. The doctor agreed to my request on the condition that my attendance at the celebration be brief. Most importantly, I was not to touch or kiss anybody due to my now-suppressed immune system.

At the party, I discovered great kindness and support from so many friends. This was the beginning of my real rehabilitation.

Life thereafter started to include me again and I ventured out a little more each day. Though I was afraid of falling, I made it a point to enjoy the outside world daily, if only briefly. Gradually—and without warning—a new normalcy returned.

I had put my trust in God and he had answered my prayers. Having been so near to death, I was now in good health, full of vitality, minus alcohol, of course.

⊰ 26 ⊱

An Ordinary Couple

A TERRIBLE RECESSION HAD begun in 2008. The design
world essentially crumbled and the real estate market took a nose-
dive. I was only working on small jobs. Money was tight and even the
wealthy were not spending wildly anymore. The stock market plum-
meted. Fortunately, we had always saved, so we got by, even with Orin
in retirement.

In 2010, we were still living at Glen Towers. We had gone through
both good and bad times there. We'd lost Cristal in 2006, and gotten
married in 2008. I'd survived my liver transplant and, unknown to us
at the time, we were about to start an exciting new chapter in our life.

One day Jay called and said he had something important to tell
us. We all sat down in our living room while Jay, with slow dramatic
intent, stated that *An Ordinary Couple* had been accepted to screen
at the Outfest Film Festival in Los Angeles. We were blown away. Not
knowing about the festival in great detail, we simply said yes, and ran
with this opportunity.

In May 2010, *An Ordinary Couple* premiered at the Director's
Guild and the Sunset Laemmle cinema in West Hollywood. Both

screenings were sold out. Never one to miss an opportunity to celebrate, I decided to have a post-screening party poolside on the grounds of our condo complex. We invited everyone who had participated in the production as well as our friends and family who had attended this premiere screening. There was entertainment, cocktails and hors d'oeuvres were served, and the response was so very positive. Finally, *An Ordinary Couple* had reached the big screen after six years in the making and just two months after my transplant.

There were necessary legalities that had to be formalized if we were to pursue distribution of our film. We hired a lawyer and assigned ourselves to be partners with Jay and Susan. After this rather arduous legal ordeal, we received more offers to screen the film at festivals.

Following its premiere in Los Angeles, we received an invitation to screen from the SHOUT Film Festival in Birmingham, Alabama. Since it was my hometown, we were offered free airline and hotel accommodations. We received a wonderful reception, winning both Best Documentary as well as the Audience Choice Awards. Plenty of Alabama friends and of course my sister Marietta and my niece Mellisa and their families attended. They were overwhelmed and loved the film. They all loved the film.

Next stop was the Ft. Lauderdale International Film Festival in Florida. Again, we won the Audience Choice Award and Orin's family was able to attend. The reception was so wonderful that we decided to spend a week reveling in our success, being invited to parties and luncheons, and meeting great people.

The NewFest Film Festival in New York City and the Austin Film Festival followed. The *Austin Chronicle* review was especially kind, stating, "It's the story itself that packs the punch, and this couple's story can't help but be extraordinary."

Throughout all of this, I was still in rehabilitation mode, but with each successful festival, my health seemed to rebound with renewed strength and vitality. After having such a major surgery and surviving, it really seemed like I had a completely *new* vision of my life. Having the movie travel all over the country also gave me such amazing confidence and a positive attitude that Orin and I had made a tremendous difference in not only our lives, but so many people's lives. As I say in the film, I will always be me! A very proud gay man.

Our greatest triumph, in my opinion, was a screening at Cinema Diverse in Palm Springs, California, to a predominantly gay audience. It sold out in advance. We were greeted with unprecedented adulation. This festival rescreened our film, based on its past success, in 2015.

Despite many years of touring festivals with *An Ordinary Couple*, I had misgivings. In truth, I felt the film was never completed. As executive producer, I added several important additions to the film, including my liver transplant and the US Supreme Court ruling on gay marriage—two major issues I insisted would enhance the audience's film experience, both on a factual and emotional level, adding guts to the film. I proved to be correct. The changes turned a very ordinary documentary into an award-winning documentary that I'm very proud of, making a tremendous difference—especially with our audiences all over the country—and making it a real story of survival. *An Ordinary Couple* became a love story of personal survival, in many ways leaving audiences rapt and emotionally affected. Film festival offers continued to come our way.

The real estate market started to rebound. I decided to sell Glen Towers while I still could. I prepared the property for viewing, something I always did because I had so much stuff—too much of everything. I had to store several pieces of furniture and remove excess accessories.

Orin agreed with this enterprise, but I didn't think he really wanted to sell. He never believed I would get my asking price. Nor did the realtors. I knew differently. My philosophy was that it only took one person to buy the place. After four weeks, that was exactly what happened.

After six or seven showings—all of which I attended—I made

a deal. The buyer was general manager of a major luxury hotel in Beverly Hills. Orin was pleasingly surprised with the transaction, as was the realtor.

It proved to be a million-dollar profit, and you can only imagine how thrilled I was at this particular accomplishment. Now I'm ready to do it again. God willing.

At this point in my life, Orin and I decided that a much-needed vacation was warranted. We embarked on a fabulous three-week trip to Europe with our good friends from Dallas, Steve and Deborah Goldstein.

Upon our return, while searching the Internet on a Saturday, Orin found a condo for sale at the Dorchester on the Wilshire Corridor. He immediately told me. I called the listing agent, and made arrangements to see the property the next day, Sunday. I knew immediately, after walking through the space, it was perfect for us. The condo had been staged. Everything was new, in color tones of grey and white, and in move-in condition for the average buyer, but not me. After we toured the unit, I said to the realtor, who I had known for years, that I wanted to make an offer. The condo was priced really well, in fairly good condition, and under a million dollars. I wanted this place, but I knew purchasing it wasn't going to be easy. The realtor told me there was lots of interest in the unit, and this was the first day on the market. He said I should make an offer, which I did that very day.

Orin and I went home and anxiously waited for a call back. Monday morning the realtor called and said, "Bernardo, we have a major problem. Can you come to my office and talk?" We were there in a couple of hours. The realtor explained he had two other offers on the condo, all cash, at full asking price with a ten-day escrow. Hearing this, I became crazed. I already told the realtor I wanted the unit and under no condition would I give it up. Then I told Orin to leave the office. He was always ready to depart when I was negotiating. I sat down at the desk.

"We have a problem," he repeated. "I have two other offers on the table."

Without showing me the offers, he mentioned one was from a Chinese entrepreneur who wanted to buy it for his daughter as a summer home. The other offer was from an Iranian exporter who wanted it for his mother-in-law. I felt my blood pressure about to explode. I needed a double vodka, but of course, I did not drink one!

I took a deep breath, looked directly at the realtor, and said in a tough Sicilian voice, "You can tell the Emperor of China and the Shah of Iran to go fuck themselves, because the Queen of Beverly Hills just bought the condo for fifty thousand dollars more than the asking price, with a ten-day escrow." The realtor, whose name I won't mention, stood up, looked at me, and said, "Can you do that?"

I said, "You bet your ass. I just did!"

The realtor appeared overwhelmed. I continued, "Don't ever underestimate me." In the end, he received a double commission.

Orin and I were thrilled with our new home. Now it was time to design and decorate our new showplace. Then we would live happily ever after or until I found something better.

We moved in October 2013 and of course I set out to make the place completely ours. Aside from the customary painting, replacing flooring, and updating the kitchen and baths, I incorporated a small third bedroom into the living area, creating a large dining room. The whole living space measured sixty feet in length.

In June of 2016, we were notified of renewed interest in *An Ordinary Couple* and were invited to screen at the Gulf Coast Film Festival in Houston, where to our great astonishment we won the top prize—Best of Festival. Our Texas friends were there to share in our success. We departed Houston with a large Oscar-like gold statuette celebrating this latest victory.

A call from Orin's high school friend Glo Klarich, from Knoxville, Tennessee, initiated what would be a first of many—a screening of *An Ordinary Couple* as a charity fundraiser. Our documentary was honored at a Positively Living event benefiting the challenges created by HIV/AIDS.

Back home, I began work on having a local theater screening of our documentary now that it had been re-edited with new footage. After numerous back-and-forth negotiations with a Beverly Hills venue, it just wasn't going to work out. I was so disappointed. Months of planning and expectation fell apart.

Periodically we attended the gay-friendly All Saints Episcopal church in Beverly Hills. We enjoyed their beautiful choir at Easter and Christmas services. Even my Jewish husband of almost ten years, Orin, enjoyed the friendly reception we received from the clergy and congregation. We attended several functions in the rectory and sanctuary, including a performance by the Three Tenors. We enjoyed their fabulous voices and the church acoustics were sublime.

I entered the church that evening feeling somewhat depressed from the disappointment of not having a Beverly Hills screening booked. As I listened to these three fabulous voices, I became overwhelmed. I felt like God spoke to me. I looked at Orin and said, "This is where we should have our next screening." He gave me that *Here we go again* look, and then simply said, "Okay," not knowing how serious I felt about it. We left the church feeling uplifted, having enjoyed the Tenors wonderful performance.

The next week we were walking out of Café D'Etoile, one of the few predominantly gay restaurants in LA that we frequented for lunch, and ran into a priest we knew from All Saints, Steve Huber. We stopped to exchange greetings. He mentioned he'd heard about our documentary, and would we consider screening it as a fundraiser for the church. I was shocked at this surprise invitation. Was it providence or coincidence?

I said, "Steve, let me think about it. I'll get back to you."

It didn't take me long to make a decision. I called Steve a few days later and said I would be thrilled and honored to screen our film, but would he entertain the idea of bringing in the Gay Men's Chorus of Los Angeles to round out a special event?

He said, "Bernardo, I know what you can do, so just do it!"

After months of planning and meetings, the day finally arrived, February 3, 2018. We had a sold-out audience of over four hundred guests. What a night! The extended applause at the film's end, in the high vaulted sanctuary, was deafening. Special effects by Images by Lighting, using primary colors, enhanced the interior as well as the exterior of the church. Everyone seemed overwhelmed by the spectacle, especially me. We received lots of great comments, applause—even bravos. It was a magnificent evening.

A celebratory VIP cocktail reception followed in the adjacent Sweetland Hall. Orin and I were deluged with compliments. We ended the evening having a late supper with Rev. Steve, who was soon to retire from the church to his home in Palm Springs.

A time to remember in a Beverly Hills church that for one night only became a grand theater.

I embrace tomorrow with customary curiosity and, I believe, courage.

Life is limitless as long as you have faith and imagination.

⊰Conclusion⊱

I TAKE THIS TIME to reflect back on my life—what I'd enjoyed, who I loved, and what I survived. The journey thus far had been profoundly adventurous and rewarding. A more philosophical question presents itself now. When I depart this world one day, will I have left it more beautiful than when I was born into it?

I pondered the question in earnest. In conclusion, I do wish to acknowledge and admit—and even declare proudly—that, yes, I have made a difference. I have touched many lives with my particular talent as an interior designer. I have loved and lost. Many friends have departed this plane of existence before me—so much sadness but so much joy as well. Life is difficult. Whoever tells you differently is either lying or selling something. If we endure, we are telling god that we continue to try, to do better, to make his universe a better place at the end of the day.

I never relied on other people to do what I could do. Because when you do it yourself and make mistakes, you can only blame yourself. In that case, you do it again and this time do it right. I learned to be strong and forceful in everything that I do and say. Also, if I don't have anything to say, I remain quiet. However, my mind never stops going—until the next idea comes into my brain. I never stop learning, listening, and watching. Those possessed of a sense of artistry are notoriously difficult. They can be downright insufferable with their attitude and behavior. They are born rebels. I was no exception to this rule of artistic entitlement. I say this with little pride—only with a sense of certainty, which is uncontestable. As I consider myself an artist—and came to that realization early in life—I know of my inherent bitchiness. With that virtue or vice, I also recognized myself to be a perfectionist. I loved beauty. Craved it. Created it. Revered it. It is what made me the successful designer I would become within the span of only a few decades. It is that sense of perfectionism which allowed me to sustain my career for fifty years.

Now, that being said, let me further state: I'm the most difficult person I've ever known. That characteristic has sometimes been a strain on those who have loved me—or whom I have loved.

This life I've led has been one of survival—and I characterize this memoir as a testimonial to that survival. I hope above all that it shall serve as a great example of one's life in so many different ways.

Growing up in small town Ensley, Alabama, was so completely different from anywhere else. Most children would have been terrified but, because my mother and grandfather were so protective and supportive, I learned to accept my differences. It was extremely difficult for me during my early school years. I was called "pretty boy" as well as other derogatory names. As I grew older, I came to accept my looks. I started exercising and built up my body as well as my self-confidence. I became steadfast in my career as an interior designer and my personal life.

As a young gay man in the late '60s, I left the South during a period of great discrimination to go to California where I could be myself. I confronted so many of life's issues that came my way, especially the abuse of alcohol, which resulted in my having a liver transplant in order to live.

I escaped the onslaught of a horrible disease, AIDS, as did Orin. I watched dozens of friends die from this disease, not truly knowing what was happening. I was witness to Elizabeth Taylor standing up for those affected with this epidemic by raising awareness as well as millions of dollars to find a cure.

I am proud to be the man I am today. I have an incredible life. I had to believe that in my inner being, I could conquer anything.

I sincerely hope my story will inspire those who are experiencing serious health issues. As sick as I was, I never gave up. My belief in God never wavered.

Going through such a life-threatening ordeal, like a transplant, cancer, or any major illness, is frightening. Everyone needs to believe in something. I had God and Orin to give me strength. No one should have to go it alone. I'll always remember the wonderful friends and family who gave me lots of support and prayers. I also want to thank my therapist and friend Dr. Anita Storm for her encouragement and support in writing my memoir. Thank you. And last but not least, my partner and husband for over forty-two years, Orin Kennedy, whom I love beyond words.

This memoir is a true story of survival.

Life is beautiful. I'm so glad I made the choice to live. I'm a much better and stronger person the second time around.

The journey continues.

No endings—only new beginnings.

⇥ Appendix ⇤

A Man of Many Faces

LEAVING ALABAMA FOR California in 1968 was the biggest step of my life. After a year in Los Angeles, I realized it was the place for me to live—a place where I could truly be myself.

At an early age I remember my mother dressing me in adorable clothes like sailor suits, cowboy outfits, beautiful short pantsuits, and caps. I loved it. As you read, in my early childhood, my favorite toy was my mother's wedding gown. I guess that gave her a clue to what her son was destined to be—a lover of clothes, jewelry, and fashion in general.

After all, Mother had me in over a dozen weddings at the family's request. In retrospect, I guess that began my love for black-tie events and my favorite ensemble—the tuxedo. I just loved getting into costume! It felt like I was on stage. I would become the character. Halloween became my favorite holiday.

Of course I loved to dress in "drag"; however, I did not know what the word *drag* meant in those days.

Being a pretty boy, it was very easy to make me a pretty girl. I didn't know that my childhood pleasure would turn into a lifetime of assuming many, many faces. I just loved getting into costume! And still do!

⊰ Acknowledgements ⊱

I am grateful to all the medical professionals that gave me a second chance at life. I would not be alive today were it not for the amazing Cedars Sinai Liver Transplant team.

To Dr. Graham Woolf and Dr. Ronald Karlsberg who supported me, not only as doctors, but friends as well, throughout the years.

A very special thanks to Dr. Anita Storm who patiently listened and encouraged me to write the story of my life.

I would like to express my gratitude to David Levishon for his splendid cover photo which he offered without my even asking.

Thank you Pamela Long for the copy edit.

Finally, my thanks and appreciation to everyone who touched my life and supported my endeavors.